READER'S DELIGHT

Communication Skills

STEPLADDERS TO SUCCESS WITH EFFECTIVE COMMUNICATION

by

PETER SIMON

READER'S DELIGHT

AN IMPRINT OF RAMESH PUBLISHING HOUSE

NEW DELHI

ISBN 978-81-7812-695-1

Published by: Alok Kumar Gupta *for* Reader's Delight
(An Imprint of Ramesh Publishing House)

Admin. Office: 12-H, New Daryaganj Road, Opp. Officers' Mess,
New Delhi-110002 ✆ 23275224, 23245124

Showroom: • Balaji Market, Nai Sarak, Delhi-6 ✆ 23253720, 23282525
• 4457, Nai Sarak, Delhi-6 ✆ 23918938

E-Mail: info@rameshpublishinghouse.com
For Online Shopping: www.rameshpublishinghouse.com

13th Edition: February, 2025

Printed at: Deepak Offset, Delhi

Price: Rs. 140/- only

A-62

Contents

Preface

The man spends most of his time receiving and conveying information that is communicating. Communication has been accompanying us from the very beginning. The word "communication" originates from the Latin word *"communicare"*, which means to share, discuss, deliberate, and ask for advice. This book provides strong evidence that leadership is not only a leader's matter - it is a matter of concern for the whole leadership community. Within early childhood education this means that the stakeholders, including centre staff, have a strong influence on leadership. Yet, a leader has to develop her/his leadership skills, like interpersonal communication, in order to "cope with the every day challenges of leadership, management and administration.

There is truly no other activity which is as varied as communication. There are a thousand ways and in each of them a new thousand ways. Therefore, communication is never perfect and only thus possible. It is always only one of the possibilities, yet then real and genuine. We discover new facts with it, we convey them to the others, and most importantly, we are part of this delight—the present moment orientated towards the creation of future. This book provides the resources that students and lecturers may not previously have had access to in one format and we look forward to receiving feedback for improvements to future editions. This book is meant to be a student-friendly, useful, and informal guide to help students as well as professionals become better communicators.

– Publisher

Chapter 1

Communication

INTRODUCTION

What is 'communication'? According to the Concise Oxford Dictionary the word means 'the act of imparting, especially news', or 'the science and practice of transmitting information'. These definitions clearly show the link between 'teaching' and 'communication': teachers are constantly imparting new knowledge, or transmitting information.

Communication is a complex process. At any stage of this process things may go wrong, making the communication less effective. For instance, the sender may not express what s/he wants to say clearly; or the room may be noisy; or the receiver may not understand the words the sender is using. To be effective, teachers have to try to minimise these barriers to communication. We do this in a number of ways – for example, by making sure that the room is quiet and well lit; by speaking slowly and clearly; by only using words which the students should be able to understand. However, the most important way to overcome the barriers is two-way communication. This means getting regular feedback from the receivers— Are they really understanding what we are trying to put across?

This kind of communication is usually subconscious – we use it without thinking about it; that is why we say that 'it is difficult to lie in body language'. If teachers really attend to the body language of their students they will know when they are bored or confused. From the body language of their teachers students pick up whether they are confident and enthusiastic.

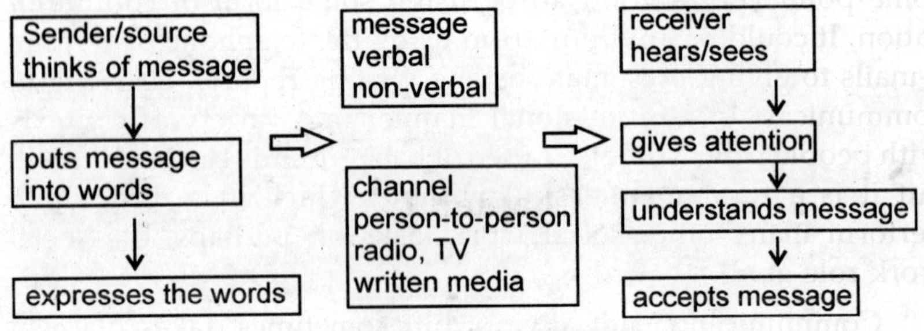

Fig. *Communication*

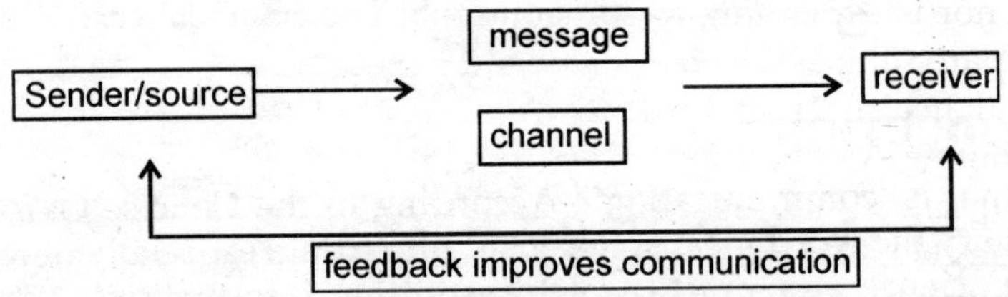

Fig. *Two-Way Communication*

Communication does not only take place by means of words; non-verbal communication (or body language) is equally important. We are all familiar with the different kinds of non-verbal communication.

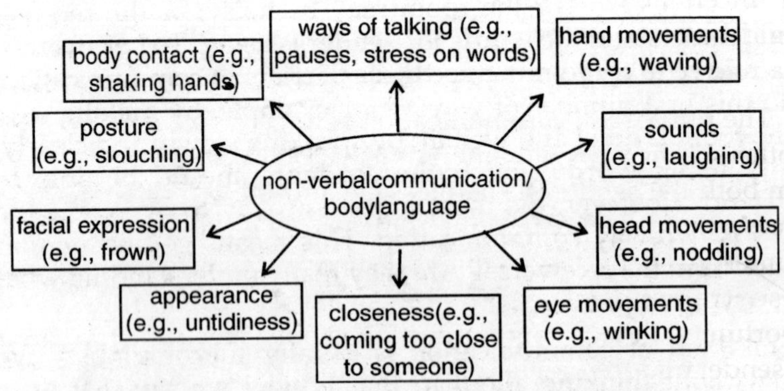

Fig. *Non-verbal Communication/Body Language*

Communication is essential to every area of life. It doesn't matter whether you're at work, in college or out socially. At some point you're going to be using some form of communication. It could be anything from using the telephone or writing e-mails to giving presentations and writing reports. Learning to communicate in a professional manner in a variety of contexts with people from a diverse range of backgrounds can be difficult, but it is a fundamental skill without which it is difficult to perform many other social work tasks or, perhaps, the social work role at all.

Communication not always, but sometimes, takes place in difficult and challenging contexts. Finding a way to engage with someone who avoids all contact with social care agencies is not easy; nor is explaining to someone that you have concerns about their parenting skills or to a career that their son is experiencing a mental health crisis and needs urgent admission to hospital. Communicating with people with different communication needs to you can also pose challenges if you do not speak the same language or know enough about their specific mode of communication or preferences.

For qualified or student social workers who are communicating with service users, careers or other professionals, or for students in simulated situations such as role play carried out in front of peers and teachers, these circumstances can conjure up a variety of uncomfortable emotions. Embarrassment, anxiety, fear and uncertainty are but a few of those emotions described. It should be of no surprise, then, that when asking for volunteers for a role play people rush to the back of the queue.

The purpose of communication is to get your message across to others clearly and unambiguously. Doing this involves effort from both the sender of the message and the receiver. And it's a process that can be fraught with error, with messages often misinterpreted by the recipient. When this isn't detected, it can cause tremendous confusion, wasted effort and missed opportunity. In fact, communication is only successful when both the sender and the receiver understand the same information as a result of the communication.

Here are a few of the more general things you might have thought of:

- Talking face-to-face with people you live with·
- Talking on the phone·
- Buying bus or train tickets·
- Going to the shops, talking to staff·
- Sending text messages from your mobile·
- Writing letters or e-mails·
- Arranging to meet friends·
- Going to interviews

By successfully getting your message across, you convey your thoughts and ideas effectively. When not successful, the thoughts and ideas that you send do not necessarily reflect your own, causing a communications breakdown and creating roadblocks that stand in the way of your goals – both personally and professionally.

In a recent survey of recruiters from companies with more than 50,000 employees, communication skills were cited as the single more important decisive factor in choosing managers. The survey, conducted by the University of Pittsburgh's Katz Business School, points out that communication skills, including written and oral presentations, as well as an ability to work with others, are the main factor contributing to job success.

In spite of the increasing importance placed on communication skills, many individuals continue to struggle, unable to communicate their thoughts and ideas effectively – whether in verbal or written format. This inability makes it nearly impossible for them to compete effectively in the workplace, and stands in the way of career progression.

Getting your message across is paramount to progressing. To do this, you must understand what your message is, what audience you are sending it to, and how it will be perceived. You must also weigh-in the circumstances surrounding your communications, such as situational and cultural context.

THE COMMUNICATION PROCESS

Problems with communication can pop-up at every stage of the communication process (which consists of sender, encoding, channel, decoding, receiver, feedback and context) and have the potential to create misunderstanding and confusion.

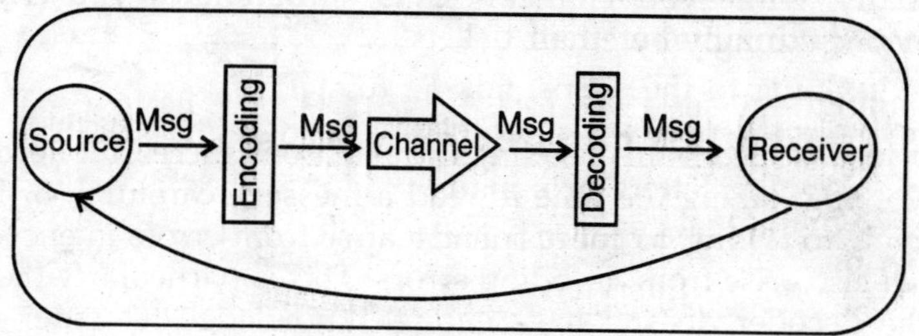

Fig. *The Communication Process*

Source

As the source of the message, you need to be clear about why you're communicating, and what you want to communicate. You also need to be confident that the information you're communicating is useful and accurate.

Message

The message is the information that you want to communicate.

Encoding

This is the process of transferring the information you want to communicate into a form that can be sent and correctly decoded at the other end. Your success in encoding depends partly on your ability to convey information clearly and simply, but also on your ability to anticipate and eliminate sources of confusion, like, cultural issues, mistaken assumptions, and missing information. A key part of this is knowing your audience: Failure to understand who you are communicating with will result in delivering messages that are misunderstood.

Channel

Messages are conveyed through channels, with verbal including face-to-face meetings, telephone and video conferencing; and written including letters, emails, memos and reports.

Different channels have different strengths and weaknesses. It's not particularly effective to give a long list of directions verbally, while you'll quickly cause problems if you criticize someone strongly by email.

Decoding

Just as successful encoding is a skill, so is successful decoding (involving, taking the time to read a message carefully, or listen actively to it.) Just as confusion can arise from errors in encoding, it can also arise from decoding errors. This is particularly the case if the decoder doesn't have enough knowledge to under-stand the message.

Receiver

Your message is delivered to individual members of your audience. No doubt, you have in mind the actions or reactions you hope your message will get from this audience. Keep in mind, though, that each of these individuals enters into the communication process with ideas and feelings that will undoubtedly influence their understanding of your message, and their response. To be a successful communicator, you should consider these before delivering your message, and act appropriately.

Feedback

Your audience will provide you with feedback, verbal and Non–verbal reactions to your communicated message. Pay close attention to this feedback, as it is the only thing that allows you to be confident that your audience has understood your message. If you find that there has been a misunderstanding, at least you have the opportunity to send the message a second time.

Context

The situation in which your message is delivered is the context. This may include the surrounding environment or broader culture (i.e. corporate culture, international cultures, etc.).

Stages

To deliver your messages effectively, you must commit to breaking down the barriers that exist in each of these stages of the communication process. Let's begin with the message itself.

If your message is too lengthy, disorganized, or contains errors, you can expect the message to be misunderstood and misinterpreted. Use of poor verbal and body language can also confuse the message. Barriers in context tend to stem from senders offering too much information too fast. When in doubt here, less is oftentimes more. It is best to be mindful of the demands on other people's time, especially in today's ultra-busy society. Once you understand this, you need to work to understand your audience's culture, making sure you can converse and deliver your message to people of different backgrounds and cultures within your own organization, in your country and even abroad.

□□

Chapter 2

Verbal and Non-Verbal Communication

There may be no observation about communication skills that is more fundamental, and more far-reaching in its implications, than that they are developed and refined over time through implementation. Communication skills do not appear instantaneously, fully developed, and ready to be applied in persuading, comforting, or understanding others. The novice public speaker, interviewer, therapist, or negotiator is unlikely to be as polished or as successful as one who has a wealth of experience in such activities.

The general idea that communication skills develop gradually through use is widely recognized and accepted, so much so that it can be seen to constitute the basic warrant for much of what transpires in college courses on communication skills, professional training seminars, and relationship counselling sessions. Doubtless, most communication teachers and trainers would conclude with psychologist Michael Argyle of Nottingham UK, and his associates that "practice is essential" in the acquisition of social skills.

Experts say that communication is composed of different methods: words, voice, tone and non-verbal clues. Of these, some are more effective in delivering a message than others. According to research, in a conversation or verbal exchange:

- Words are seven percent effective
- Tone of voice is 38 percent effective
- Non-verbal clues are 55 percent effective.

Most people fail to realise that a great deal of our communication is of a Non–verbal form. Non-verbal communication includes facial expressions, eye contact, body posture and motions (e.g. arms crossed, standing, sitting, relaxed, tense), and positioning within groups. It may also include the way we wear our clothes or the silence we keep. WHAT you say is not nearly as important as HOW you say it. A dull message delivered by a charismatic person, filled with energy and enthusiasm will be accepted as brilliant. An excellent message delivered by someone who is not interested in the topic will not engage the enthusiasm of its intended audience. In person-to-person communications our messages are sent on two levels simultaneously. If the non-verbal cues and the spoken message are incongruous, the flow of communication is hindered. Rightly or wrongly, the receiver of the communication tends to base the intentions of the sender on the non-verbal cues he or she receives. Knowledge of non-verbal communication is important when dealing with a difficult or potentially violent situation with a family member who has a dual diagnosis.

- Picking up on the early non-verbal cues in a difficult situation will mean that you are better equipped to handle that situation.
- By understanding the non-verbal communication, you will be able to respond to someone in a way that is more appropriate to their communication style.
- Having knowledge of non-verbal cues may also enable you to act in such a way as to prevent a potentially violent situation from escalating any further.

If you show a true awareness to non-verbal cues, you will have a better chance of a successful interaction in a difficult or potentially violent situation.

STATIC FEATURES OF NON–VERBAL COMMUNICATION THAT PROVIDE INFORMATION

Distance

The distance one person stands from another frequently conveys a non-verbal message. In some cultures it is a sign of attraction, while in others it may reflect status or the intensity of the exchange.

Personal Space

Personal space is your 'bubble' – the space you place between yourself and others. This invisible boundary becomes apparent only when someone bumps or tries to enter your bubble. How you identify your personal space and use the environment in which you find yourself influences your ability to send or receive messages. How close do you stand to the one with whom you are communicating? Where do you sit in the room? All of these things affect your level of comfort, and the level of comfort of those receiving your message.

Orientation

People may present themselves in various ways: face-to-face, side-to-side, or even back-to-back. For example, cooperating people are likely to sit side-by-side while competitors frequently face one another.

Posture

People can be lying down, seated, or standing. These are not the elements of posture that convey messages. Are we slouched or erect? Are our legs crossed or our arms folded? Such postures convey a degree of formality or relaxation in the communication exchange.

Physical Contact

Shaking hands, touching, holding, embracing, pushing, or patting on the back all convey messages. They reflect an element of intimacy or a feeling of (or lack of) attraction.

DYNAMIC FEATURES OF NON-VERBAL COMMUNICATION THAT PROVIDE INFORMATION

Facial Expressions

A smile, frown, raised eyebrow, yawn, and sneer all convey information. Facial expressions continually change during interaction and are monitored constantly by the recipient. There is evidence that the meaning of these expressions may be similar across cultures.

Gestures

One of the most frequently observed, but least understood cues, is a hand movement. Most people use hand movements regularly when talking. While some gestures (e.g. a clenched fist) have universal meanings, most of the others are individually learned and idiosyncratic.

Looking

A major feature of social communication is eye contact. It can convey emotion or aversion, and signal when to talk or finish. The frequency of contact may suggest either interest or boredom.

OTHER IMPORTANT ASPECTS OF COMMUNICATION THAT PROVIDE INFORMATION

Paralanguage

Is the content of your message contradicted by the attitude with which you are communicating it? Researchers have found that the tone, pitch, quality of voice, and rate of speaking convey emotions that can be accurately judged regardless of the content of the message. The important thing is that the voice is important, not just as the conveyor of the message, but as a complement to the message. As a communicator, you should be sensitive to the influence of tone, pitch, and quality of your voice on the interpretation of your message by the receiver.

Silence And Time

Silence can be a positive or negative influence in the communications process. It can provide a link between messages, or sever relationships. It can create tension and uneasiness or create a peaceful situation. Silence can also be judgmental by indicating favour or disfavour, agreement or disagreement. For example, by remaining silent when someone is displaying non-verbal cues of violence/anger you may avoid aggravating the situation and may actually prevent it from escalating.

Be Aware

It is important for you to develop some sensitivity to non-verbal messages. Cooperation and communication improves as we recognize and respond appropriately to non-verbal cues. You have been aware of non-verbal communications all your life, but how much thought have you given them?

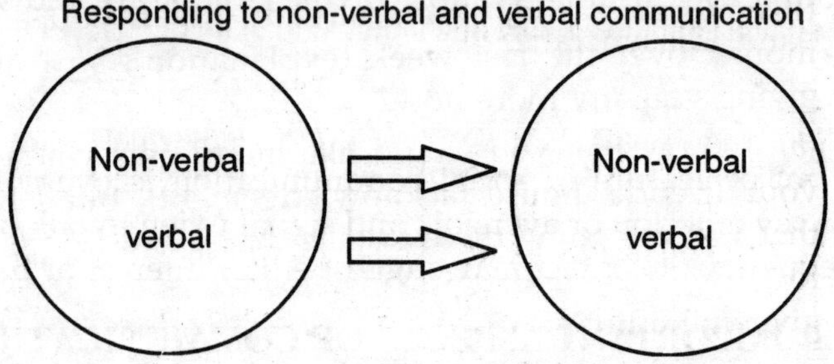

Fig. *Non-verbal communication needs to be matched with non-verbal communication. Verbal communication needs to be matched with verbal communication*

SAYING 'NO': A GUIDE TO SETTING LIMITS

At times it is difficult to say 'no' to requests that you do not want to meet. Saying 'no' means that you set limits on other people's demands for your time and energy when such demands conflict with your needs and desires. It also means that you can do this without feeling guilty. In some cases, just saying 'no' or 'I'm not interested' in a polite, firm manner should suffice. If the other person persists, just repeat your statement without apologizing. The form of communication needs to be matched with its own form.

RESPONDING TO NON-VERBAL AND VERBAL COMMUNICATION

If you need to make your statement stronger and more emphatic, you may want to (1) look the person in the eye, (2) raise the level of your voice slightly and (3) assert your position – 'I said no'.

Three Step Procedure For Saying 'No'

- Acknowledge the other person's request by repeating it.
- Explain your reason for declining it.
- Say 'No'.

  Examples: (*a*) 'I know that you would like me to give you Rs. 200 (acknowledgement), but I gave you Rs. 200 this morning and I have already given you a lot of money over the last week (explanation), so I am not giving you any more now.'

  (*b*) 'I know that you would like me to give you a lift to your friend's house (acknowledgement), but I believe that you are going there to take drugs and I don't want to support your drug-taking (explanation), so I won't give you a lift.'

Important Points To Remember

- ***Take your time:*** If you are the type of person who has difficulty saying 'no', give yourself some time to think and clarify what you want to say before responding to someone's request. *Example:* 'I will let you know by the end of the day.'
- ***Do not over-apologise:*** When you apologise to people for saying 'no', you give them the message that you are not sure that your own needs are as important as their's. This opens the door for them to put more pressure on you to comply with what they want. In some cases, they may even try to play upon your guilt to obtain other things or to get you to 'make it up to them' for having said 'no' in the first place.
- ***Be specific:*** It is important to be very specific in stating what you will and will not do. *Example:* 'I won't give you money for cigarettes but I can take you to the shop and buy some for you.'
- ***Use assertive body language:*** Be sure to face the person you are talking to squarely and maintain good eye contact. Work on speaking in a calm but firm tone of voice. Avoid becoming emotional.

- ***Watch out for guilt:*** You may feel the impulse to do something else for someone after turning down his or her request. Take your time before offering to do so. Make sure that your offer comes out of genuine desire rather than guilt.

CONVEYING AND INTERPRETING COMMUNICATION

Non–verbal communication is a silent infiltrator, having broad influence over our social environment. It provides us with a mode for conveying messages without the use of verbal language. It may enhance or detract from a verbal communication. It regulates relationships by affecting the likelihood of introduction and continued interaction. We are able to infer emotion through non–verbal communication and influence other's perception of our competence, power and vulnerability. It also plays a role in the perception of the actual message we are trying to convey. It affects our lives in a myriad of ways from childhood throughout adulthood, and as long as we intend to communicate with others.

Communication is a dynamic process with the interacting components of sending, receiving and feedback. Non–verbal cues may provide clarity or contradiction for a message being sent. If an ironic statement is made with a smile, the receiver knows to find it humorous instead of disconcerting. If we are sending a verbal message intending to deceive and avert our eyes the receiver knows we may be lying. Non–verbal cues also influence how we perceive and are perceived. Familiar faces may make us more likely to start a relationship and continue it. Nervous facial expression hinders other's perception of our competence and persuasiveness. Non–verbal cues can provide information we may not want dispelled. Our decoding ability arises at a young age and increases as we get older, influencing our daily lives whether we are aware of it or not.

Non–verbal communication has many functions in the communication process. It regulates relationships and may support or replace verbal communication. Among the many factors contributing to non–verbal communication are sending and receiving ability and accuracy, perception of appropriate social roles, and cognitive desire for interpersonal involvement or assessment. Difficulties may arise if communicators are unaware of the types of messages they are sending and how the receiver is interpreting those messages. Discrepancy may also arise if the sender's message does not fit the receiver's perception of social norms for the particular situation. All parties involved must desire interaction in order for reciprocal communication to occur. Research in non–verbal communication provides awareness and possible solutions to many communication problems.

The ambiguous nature of emotion creates a wide variety of possible interpretations for both sender and receiver. Our ability to non–verbally communicate accurately is inhibited by internal and external properties. Humans do not display pure emotion. Our affective states are a mixture of varying quantities and strength of emotion. The neurophysiologic composition of the human body defines our ability to convey opposing and overlapping emotions at the same time. For example, anger, is often accompanied by anxiety and fear. The emotional overlap often creates confusing messages for the receiver. Generally there is not a thorough understanding of our own affect states. Studies have shown a few emotions, happiness, sadness, anger and fear can be distinguished cross-culturally.

In general humans are able to communicate complex emotion through behavioural cues allowing the recipient opportunity to infer the sender's prevailing psychological state. The vocalization and context of the experienced emotion are integral components to the accurate expression and interpretation of the sender's affective state. It is possible, however, to decode a sender's conveyed emotion relying on non–verbal cues only. When the behavioural cue is out of context there is less emotion decoding accuracy. Communication is not a static event. It implies sending, receiving and feedback. Emotional expression is a communication process. By choosing one emotional message cue, as is often done in the experimental setting, disregarding previous and subsequent messages may negate the overall intended communication.

The ability to interpret non–verbal communication is acquired at a very young age. Triadic eye gaze was considered in a study addressing the age at which children are able to infer a sender's desire. Results showed a two-year-old child is able to identify the direction of the eye gaze and to what specific object or person the gaze is referring. Other non–verbal cues like pointing and dyadic eye gaze are used by children from an even earlier age. This early onset of non–verbal communication ability highlights the importance of understanding another's desires.

How much ability is due to an innate developmental process or learning has yet to be decided. Whatever the cause, it provides children with one mode among many for conveying internal desires and understanding others without the use of verbal communication. As we grow older our non–verbal communication ability increases.

PERSON TO PERSON COMMUNICATION

When we communicate with each other, we run great risks. Misunderstandings and unintended offenses are just some of the ways person-to-person communication can go wrong.

Core Message:

- Person-to-person communications are complex
- Problems that do arise are difficult to fix
- Preventing problems is easier than repairing them
- We have little control over how others interpret what we communicate
- For best results, prevent problems by changing our inner processes

Communication and appearance are our ways of expressing to the world what we really are. In theory, we have total control of the message we are sending.

In reality, most of our communicative messages get added to: involuntary body movements, the tone of voice and physical appearance load the message with extra content and structure, telling more about us that we initially wanted it to. In theory, the tools we use for communication can bring us quite close to the original, i.e. face-to-face context.

If the receiving interface handles incoming messages differently from how they are intended to, the receiver will most likely be dissatisfied in the user interface. Communication depends as much on receiving what is sent, as delivering what is intended. Asymmetry in how messages are handled affects how the medium is used in communication and thus unreliable handling of incoming messages limits the potential of the developing communication culture. People will not want to send messages if they aren't sure their recipients' user interfaces are able to receive them. Picture messages, for instance, have not made any great success, as some mobile phones cannot handle them.

□□

Chapter 3

Communication Skills in Theory and Practice

BASIC COMMUNICATION SKILLS

Communication is a two-way process between a sender of information and a receiver of information. To be effective, communication involves the use of four skills:

- Leveling
- Listening
- Validating
- 'I…' statements

Leveling

Effective communication can only occur when both parties know all the relevant information (thoughts, feeling and facts). It is wrong to expect others to know what is on our minds. Misunderstanding and conflict commonly arise because one party does not know important information. Leveling means giving the other person information about your thoughts and feelings, rather than expecting her or him to read your mind. It is also important to regularly check that the other person has understood what it is you are saying. Essentially, this skill is the development of a level playing field in all interpersonal interactions.

Listening

This skill not only involves hearing but actively processing what others say. This requires directing our attention to what others say rather than what we are going to say next.

Validating

This skill involves communicating to others that you have heard their position or opinion. It is not necessary to understand or agree with them, but it is important to recognize and accept their rights to feel and think as they do. It is important to accept that what others say about how they are feeling is true.

'I...' Statements

When you communicate how you feel to someone, are making a request, or saying 'no' to a demand, begin what you say with the expression 'I'. In this way you take responsibility for your wants and feelings rather than putting them on to the other person, which can lead to defensiveness and hostility.

An example of these communication techniques...

"I feel worried and frustrated when you don't take your medication because it is an important aspect in the management of your illness ('I' statement). I understand that you may have concerns about the side-effects of the medication (validation) and I am here to support you and listen if you need someone to talk to (willingness to listen)".

COMMUNICATION IS INDIVIDUAL

We're Not All The Same

When you look at communication, presentation skills are not all there is to it. Far from it, everyone communicates differently and sees the world differently. The greatest skill you can have in order to instantly and significantly improve you communications skills is to understand the other person's point view and how they see the world. Then you can adjust your own communication to take that into account.

Change Yourself To Change Others

Alongside this has to be the knowledge that the only person you can be sure of changing in any communication is you. Therefore, the most effective way to be in charge of what happens in any communication dynamic is changing what you do. When you can do this you are well on the way to promoting better relationships.

You Are The Only One Of You

There's never one right way to communicate. Authentic effective communication always happens when we reply on those things we know to be true about or for ourselves. Remember your personal style probably says more for you than all the words you use can.

What's Already Working?

Most people tend to look at what's wrong with themselves and other people rather than focusing on what already works. Remember, something (more than one thing, of course) has to be working well for you to have got this far already!

Barriers To Effective Communication

There are a wide number of sources of noise or interference that can enter into the communication process. This can occur when people know each other very well and should understand the sources of error. In a work setting, it is even more common since interactions involve people who not only lack years of experience with each other, but communication is complicated by the complex and often conflicting relationships that exist at work. In a work setting, the following suggests a number of sources of noise:

- ***Language:*** The choice of words or language in which a sender encodes a message will influence the quality of communication. Because language is a symbolic representation of a phenomenon, room for interpretation and distortion of the meaning exists. In the above example, the Boss uses language (this is the third day you've missed) that is likely to convey far more than objective information. To John it conveys indifference to his medical problems. Note that the same words will be interpreted different by each different person. Meaning has to be given to words and many factors affect how an individual will attribute meaning to particular words. It is important to note that no two people will attribute the exact same meaning to the same words.

- Defensiveness, distorted perceptions, guilt, project, transference, distortions from the past
- Misreading of body language, tone and other non-verbal forms of communication
- Noisy transmission (unreliable messages, inconsistency)
- Receiver distortion: selective hearing, ignoring non-verbal cues
- Power struggles
- Self-fulfilling assumptions
- Language—different levels of meaning
- Managers hesitation to be candid
- Assumptions—e.g. assuming others see situation same as you, has same feelings as you
- Distrusted source, erroneous translation, value judgment, state of mind of two people

• ***Perceptual Biases:*** People attend to stimuli in the environment in very different ways. We each have shortcuts that we use to organize data. Invariably, these shortcuts introduce some biases into communication. Some of these shortcuts include stereotyping, projection, and self-fulfilling prophecies. Stereotyping is one of the most common. This is when we assume that the other person has certain characteristics based on the group to which they belong without validating that they in fact have these characteristics.

• ***Interpersonal Relationships:*** How we perceive communication is affected by the past experience with the individual. Perception is also affected by the organizational relationship two people have. For example, communication from a superior may be perceived differently than that from a subordinate or peer.

• ***Cultural Differences:*** Effective communication requires deciphering the basic values, motives, aspirations, and assumptions that operate across geographical lines. Given some dramatic differences across cultures in approaches to such areas as time, space, and privacy, the opportunities for miscommunication while we are in cross-cultural situations are plentiful.

Characteristics Of Effective Feedback

Effective Feedback has most of the following characteristics:

- Descriptive (not evaluative)(avoids defensiveness.) By describing one's own reactions, it leaves the individual free to use it or not to use it as he sees fit.
- Avoid accusations; present data if necessary.
- Describe your own reactions or feelings; describe objective consequences that have or will occur; focus on behaviour and your own reaction, not on other individual or his or her attributes.
- Suggest more acceptable alternative; be prepared to discuss additional alternatives; focus on alternatives.
- Specific rather than general.
- Focused on behaviour not the person. It is important that we refer to what a person does rather than to what we think he is. Thus we might say that a person "talked more than anyone else in this meeting" rather than that he is a "loud-mouth."
- It takes into account the needs of both the receiver and giver of feedback. It should be given to help, not to hurt. We too often give feedback because it makes us feel better or gives us a psychological advantage.
- It is directed toward behaviour which the receiver can do something about. A person gets frustrated when reminded of some shortcoming over which he has no control.
- It is solicited rather than imposed. Feedback is most useful when the receiver himself has formulated the kind of question which those observing him can answer or when he actively seeks feedback.
- Feedback is useful when well-timed (soon after the behaviour—depending, of course, on the person's readiness to hear it, support available from others, and

so forth). Excellent feedback presented at an inappropriate time may do more harm than good.

- Sharing of information, rather than giving advice allows a person to decide for himself, in accordance with his own goals and needs. When we give advice we tell him what to do, and to some degree take away his freedom to decide for himself.
- It involves the amount of information the receiver can use rather than the amount we would like to give. To overload a person with feedback is to reduce the possibility that he may be able to use what he receives effectively. When we give more than can be used, we are more often than not satisfying some need of our own rather than helping the other person.
- It concerns what is said and done, or how, not why. The "why" involves assumptions regarding motive or intent and this tends to alienate the person generate resentment, suspicion, and distrust. If we are uncertain of his motives or intent, this uncertainty itself is feedback, however, and should be revealed.
- It is checked to insure clear communication. One way of doing this is to have the receiver try to rephrase the feedback. No matter what the intent, feedback is often threatening and thus subject to considerable distortion or misinterpretation.
- It is checked to determine degree of agreement from others. Such "consensual validation" is of value to both the sender and the receiver.
- It is followed by attention to the consequences of the feedback. The supervisor needs to become acutely aware of the effects of his feedback.
- It is an important step toward authenticity. Constructive feedback opens the way to a relationship which is built on trust, honest, and genuine concern and mutual growth.

Part of the feedback process involves understanding and predicting how the other person will react. Or, in the case of our receiving feedback, we need to understand ways that we respond to feedback, especially threatening feedback.

People often react negatively to threatening feedback. This reaction can take a number of forms including:

- Selective reception and selective perception
- Doubting motive of the giver
- Denying validity of the data
- Rationalizing
- Attack the giver of the data

Following the guidelines to effective feedback can go a long way to limit these kinds of reactions but we need to be conscious of them nonetheless and be ready to react appropriately. When we are on the receiving end of feedback we should be careful to avoid these pitfalls. Try to keep these points in mind.

- Try not to be defensive
- Check on possible misunderstanding ("Let me restate what I am hearing")
- Gather information from other sources
- Don't overreact
- Ask for clarification

□□

Chapter 4

Interpersonal Skills

Interpersonal skills refer to mental and communicative algorithms applied during social communications and interactions in order to reach certain effects or results. The term "interpersonal skills" is used often in business contexts to refer to the measure of a person's ability to operate within business organizations through social communication and interactions. An interpersonal skill is how a person relates to one another. As an illustration, it is generally understood that communicating respect for other people or professionals within the workplace will enable one to reduce conflict and increase participation or assistance in obtaining information or completing tasks.

For instance, in order to interrupt someone who is currently preoccupied with a task in order to obtain information needed immediately, it is recommended that a professional utilize a deferential approach with language such as, "Excuse me, are you busy? I have an urgent matter to discuss with you if you have the time at the moment". This allows the receiving professional to make their own judgment regarding the importance of their current task versus entering into a discussion with their colleague. While it is generally understood that interrupting someone with an 'urgent' request will often take priority, allowing the receiver of the message to independently judge the request and agree to further interaction will likely result in a higher quality interaction. Following these kinds of heuristics to achieve better professional results generally results in a professional being ranked as one with 'Good Interpersonal Skills'. Often these evaluations occur in formal and informal settings. This helps for the effective productivity in the organization without any conflicts.

DEVELOPING INTERPERSONAL COMMUNICATION

Developing interpersonal communication skills is vitally important in today's workplace. Even though you are an individual contributor in the workplace, you still need to communicate effectively with your boss as well as customers. Almost all kinds of work require communicating wit. Most people have colleagues with whom they need to communicate in order to be successful at their job.

When we communicate, we don't actually swap ideas, we swap symbols that stand for ideas. Words are just symbols that do not have inherent meaning; we simply use them in certain ways to convey an idea or give it a meaning, and no two people use the same word in the same sense at all instances. The symbols attached to these words are a function of who we are, our social upbringing and culture, which will pretty much vary quite widely in today's work environment.

Our personal communication skills would be largely dependant on our cultural background and unique histories. As a result, there is a real possibility that when two of us get together there are chances that we are less effective at communicating with each other than we would like.

SOME FACTS ON INTERPERSONAL COMMUNICATION

Interpersonal Communication Is Inescapable

We cannot 'not communicate'. The very attempt not to communicate communicates something. When we are not communicating i.e. when we are silent towards the other person, we are communicating silence. Silence has many meanings depending on the circumstances and cultures. In one culture, it might be a polite thing to have a long pause before answering a question while in another culture it may be considered a dumb thing or lack of intelligence.

Communication Is Not Just Spoken Words

Remember the time you were caught coming home late? Remember the look on your Mom's face? She may not have said anything verbally but we still got the message quite clearly "Grounded".

Any communication for that matter is based not just on words but also on body language, tonality, situation etc. Using these techniques, we constantly communicate with others. Even when you sleep, you communicate. Remember the basic principle of communication: people are not mind readers. Another way to put this is: people judge you by your behaviour, not your intent.

Interpersonal Communication Is Irreversible

"Once a word goes out of your mouth, you can never swallow it again."

—A Russian proverb

You can't really take back something once it has been said. The effect must inevitably remain. Despite the instructions from a judge to a jury to "disregard that last statement the witness made," the lawyer knows that it can't help but make an impression on the jury. Some of the famous Murphy Laws on communication go this way:

- If communication can fail, it will.
- If a message can be understood in different ways, it will be understood in the way which does the most harm.
- There is always somebody who knows better than you what you meant by your message.
- The more communication there is, the more difficult it is for communication to succeed.

These tongue-in-cheek maxims are not real principles; they simply humorously remind us of the difficulty of accurate communication.

Intrapersonal Communication Is Contextual

In other words, communication does not happen in isolation. There is:

- ***A Mental context,*** which is who you are and what you bring to the interaction. Your needs, desires, values, personality, etc., all form the psychological context. ("You" here refers to both participants in the interaction.)
- ***A Relational context,*** which concerns your relations to the other person—the "mix."
- *Social context* deals with the psycho-social "where" you are communicating. An interaction that takes place in a classroom will be very different from one that takes place in a bar.
- ***Physical/Environmental context*** deals with the physical "where" you are communicating. Furniture, location, noise level, temperature, season, time of day, all are examples of factors in the environmental context.
- ***Cultural context*** includes all the learned behaviours and rules that affect the interaction. If you come from a culture (foreign or within your own country) where it is considered rude to make long, direct eye contact, you will avoid eye contact out of politeness. If the other person comes from a culture where long, direct eye contact signals trustworthiness, then we have a basis for misunderstanding.

By increasing your repertoire of interpersonal communication skills, you can increase your overall effectiveness and perhaps your job satisfaction.

□□

Chapter 5

Listening and Listening Skills

Another part of learning communication skills is to strive to be an effective listener by listening attentively to what the speaker is saying. To be an effective listener, you should be able to hear the words as the speaker communicates so that you can understand the entire message. Effective listening in developing communication skills is by looking at the speaker when he is communicating, maintaining eye contact and nodding during brief pauses. Watch the speaker's facial expression to be able to completely understand the tone of the message he is conveying.

Show open attitude to the speaker through body language and attentiveness. To be an effective listener, you must be composed when relating with the speaker. In this way, they feel more accepted when they are with you. Don't fidget or frown when looking at the speaker because he is trying to get a response from you, so giving a negative attitude makes him feel defensive, insecure and not confident.

As part of developing good communication skills, it is important to ask questions during a conversation. When asking questions, use open ended questions so that it is easier for the listener to know how to answer your questions. With all the tips given, it is obvious for us to see that communication skills is not just innate, it needs to be developed and practiced.

TYPES OF LISTENING

Different situations require different types of listening. We may listen to obtain information, improve a relationship, gain appreciation for something, make discriminations, or engage in a critical evaluation.

While certain skills are basic and necessary for all types of listening (receiving, attending, and understanding), each type requires some special skills.

Informative Listening

Informative listening is the name we give to the situation where the listener's primary concern is to understand the message. Listeners are successful in so far as the meaning they assign to messages is as close as possible to that which the sender intended.

Informative listening, or listening to understand, is found in all areas of our lives. Much of our learning comes from informative listening. For example, we listen to lectures or instructions from teachers—and what we learn depends on how well we listen. In the workplace, we listen to understand new practices or procedures—and how well we perform depends on how well we listen. We listen to instructions, briefings, reports, and speeches; if we listen poorly, we aren't equipped with the information we need.

- At times, careful informative listening is crucial.
- At other times, careless listening results in only aggravation or misunderstanding.
- Whatever the case, effective informative listening demands that you concentrate squarely on the message—and know its source.

There are three key variables related to informative listening. Knowing these variables can help you begin to improve your informative listening skills; that is, you will become increasingly successful in understanding what the speaker means.

- ***Vocabulary:*** The precise relationship between vocabulary and listening has never been determined, but it is clear that increasing your vocabulary will increase your potential for better understanding. And it's never too late to improve your vocabulary. Having a genuine interest in words and language, making a conscious effort to learn new words, breaking down unfamiliar words into their component parts—all these things will help you improve your vocabulary.

Another good way to improve your vocabulary is to be sensitive to the context in which words are used. Sometimes, unfamiliar words appear with synonyms: Her attractive, *winsome* personality won us over. At other times, a contrast is drawn: He is usually quite energetic, but today he seemed *lethargic*. Occasionally, an unfamiliar word is used to summarize a situation or quality: He passed for over 200 yards, ran for 50 more, and his three punts averaged over 45 yards; he turned in a *stellar* performance.

Look for these and other contextual clues to help you learn new words and improve your vocabulary.

- ***Concentration:*** Concentration is difficult. You can remember times when another person was not concentrating on what you were saying—and you probably can remember times when you were not concentrating on something that someone was saying to you.

  An Example: Riyan interrupted her father reading the newspaper to ask, "Is it OK if I take your car over to a friend's house to spend the night? I'll be home before you go to work in the morning." Without concentrating on what she was asking, Mr Dave said, "Sure, go ahead." Several minutes later, he realised what his daughter had said. She was not coming home that night, and he had to leave the house earlier than usual the next morning. He had to drive long to the University to give a speech—and all his notes and visual aids were in his car. Fortunately for him, Riyan had left the telephone number of her friend, and he was able to retrieve his car.

  There are many reasons people don't concentrate when listening. Sometimes listeners try to divide their attention between two competing stimuli. At other times, listeners are preoccupied with something other than the speaker of the moment. Sometimes listeners are too ego-involved, or too concerned with their own needs to concentrate on the message being delivered. Or perhaps they lack curiosity, energy, or interest. Many people simply have not learned to concentrate while listening. Others just refuse to discipline themselves, lacking the motivation to accept responsibility for good listening. Concentration requires discipline, motivation, and acceptance of responsibility.

- *Memory:* Memory is an especially crucial variable to informative listening; you cannot process information without bringing memory into play. More specifically, memory helps your informative listening in three ways.
  - It allows you to recall experiences and information necessary to function in the world around you. In other words, without memory you would have no knowledge bank.
  - It establishes expectations concerning what you will encounter. You would be unable to drive in heavy traffic, react to new situations, or make common decisions in life without memory of your past experiences.
  - It allows you to understand what others say. Without simple memory of the meaning of words, you could not communicate with anyone else. Without memory of concepts and ideas, you could not understand the meaning of messages.

Relationship Listening

The purpose of relationship listening is either to help an individual or to improve the relationship between people. Therapeutic listening is a special type of relationship listening. Therapeutic listening brings to mind situations where counsellors, medical personnel, or other professionals allow a troubled person to talk through a problem. But it can also be used when you listen to friends or acquaintances and allow them to "get things off their chests". Although relationship listening requires you to listen for information, the emphasis is on understanding the other person. Following three behaviours are key to effective relationship listening.

- ***Attending:*** Much has been said about the importance of "paying attention," or "attending" behaviour. In relationship listening, attending behaviours indicate that the listener is focusing on the speaker. Non–verbal cues are crucial in relationship listening; that is, your non–verbal behaviour indicates that you are attending to the speaker—or that you aren't!

  Eye contact is one of the most important attending behaviours. Looking appropriately and comfortably at the speaker sends a message that is different from that sent by a frequent shift of gaze, staring, or looking around the room. Body positioning communicates acceptance or lack of it. Leaning forward, toward the speaker, demonstrates interest; leaning away communicates lack of interest. Head nods, smiles, frowns, and vocalized cues such as "uh huh," "I see," or "yes"—all are positive attending behaviours. A pleasant tone of voice, gentle touching, and concern for the other person's comfort are other attending behaviours.

- ***Supporting:*** Many responses have a negative or non supportive effect; for example, interrupting the speaker, changing the subject, turning the conversation toward yourself, and demonstrating a lack of concern for the other person. Giving advice, attempting to manipulate the conversation, or indicating that you consider yourself superior are other behaviours that will have an adverse effect on the relationship.

  Sometimes the best response is silence. The speaker may need a "sounding board," not a "resounding board". Wise relationship listeners know when to talk and when to just listen—and they generally listen more than they talk.

Three characteristics describe supportive listeners: (1) *discretion*—being careful about what they say and do; (2) *belief*—expressing confidence in the ability of the other person; and (3) *patience*—being willing to give others the time they need to express themselves adequately.

- ***Empathizing:*** What is empathy? It is not sympathy, which is a feeling for or about another. Nor is it apathy, which is a lack of feeling. Empathy is feeling and thinking *with* another person. The caring, empathic listener is able to go into the world of another—to see as the other sees, hear as the other hears, and feel as the other feels.

  Obviously, the person who has had more experience and lived longer stands a better chance of being an effective empathic listener. The person who has never been divorced, lost a child to death, been bankrupt, or lost a job may have a more difficult time relating to people with these problems than one who has experienced such things.

  Risk is involved with being an empathic relationship listener. You cannot be an effective empathic listener without becoming involved, which sometimes means learning more than you really want to know. But commanders can't command effectively, bosses can't supervise skillfully, and individuals can't relate interpersonally without empathy. Abraham Lincoln is reported to have said, "I feel sorry for the man who cannot feel the stripes upon the back of another". Truly, those who cannot feel *with* another person are at a disadvantage in understanding that person.

  Empathic behaviour can be learned. First, you must learn as much as you can about the other person. Second, you must accept the other person—even if you can't accept some aspects of that person's behaviour. Third, you must have the desire to be an empathic listener. And you must remember that empathy is crucial to effective relationship listening.

Appreciative Listening

Appreciative listening includes listening to music for enjoyment, to speakers because you like their style, to your choices in theater, television, radio, or film. It is the response of the listener, not be the source of the message, that defines appreciative listening. That which provides appreciative listening for one person may provide something else for another. For example, hard rock music may not be a source of appreciative listening for Jay. He would rather listen to gospel, country, jazz, or the "golden oldies".

The quality of appreciative listening depends in large part on following three factors.

- ***Presentation:*** As mentioned, Jay prefers gospel music to hard rock. But he doesn't enjoy *all* gospel. For example, he doesn't enjoy gospel music when it is presented in a "glitzy" setting—or when it is performed by someone who fails to demonstrate an understanding of the music's meaning. (It may be added that Jay usually enjoys gospel when it is off-key or poorly done—but there are exceptions, such as the time he heard a 103-year-old man sing "Amazing Grace". Never had he enjoyed it more!)

  Jay enjoys gospel music when he hears it in the little churches. He also very much enjoys presentations of gospel music on radio, on television, or in concert by well-known performers who understand its meaning.

  Jay enjoys hearing good speakers, speakers whom he admires, and speakers who have expertise. He frequently attends lectures at the University by speakers who have all three of these characteristics.

  Presentation encompasses many factors: the medium, the setting, the style and personality of the presenter. Sometimes it is our perception of the presentation, rather than the actual presentation, that most influences our listening pleasure or displeasure. Perception is an important factor in appreciative listening.

- ***Perception:*** For years, Mayank did not care to listen to jazz music. He had always believed that people like him—from a conservative rural middle class background —wouldn't like jazz. Then he started to work for a new boss—a general officer who enjoyed jazz. He admired him very much. His mind was now open to listen to jazz. His perception was changing, and he began to enjoy jazz music.

  Expectations play a large role in perception. If Mayank attends a concert under duress with no expectation of enjoying the music he may be pleasantly surprised. But he stands a lot better chance of enjoying the concert if he *expects* to enjoy it.

  Perceptions—and the expectations that drive them—have their basis in attitudes. Our attitudes determine how we react to, and interact with, the world around us. There was a time, not many years ago, when Anil did not want a personal computer (PC) in his office. He did not want to even be *around* a PC. He did not enjoy working with computers.

  Only two years ago, he started a travelling agency. Fortunately for him, his attitude toward computers changed. If only he had changed his attitude much earlier, his agency would have been doing good business as of today.

  Perceptions influence all areas of our lives. Certainly, they are crucial determinants as to whether or not we enjoy or appreciate the things we listen to. Obviously, perceptions also determine what we listen to in the first place. As said earlier, listening is selective.

- ***Previous Experience:*** The discussion of perception makes it clear that previous experience influences whether we enjoy listening to something. In some cases, we enjoy listening to things because we are experts in the area. Sometimes, however, expertise or previous experience prevents us from enjoying a presentation because we are too sensitive to imperfections. Previous experience plays a large role in appreciative listening.

Many people enjoy the sounds of large-city traffic. Perhaps their growing up in a large city was a happy experience for them. The blare of horns honking, the sound of roaring engines accelerating, even the shrill shriek of sirens piercing the air—all these things may remind them of pleasant times in their lives. They appreciate hearing these sounds.

Others, having grown up on a farm or in a small town, have learned to enjoy the sounds of nature. For them, a walk in the country produces sounds of enjoyment: the rustle of leaves in the breeze, the chirruping of birds.

Usually, if we associate a sound or other experience with pleasant memories, then we appreciate or enjoy it. However, if the sound or experience is associated with unpleasant memories, we probably will not appreciate or enjoy it.

But we can change! Remember the example of how Mayank learned to enjoy listening to jazz. We should not shut our minds to the fact that we can learn to like, enjoy, and appreciate new and different things. We can learn to be better appreciative listeners.

Critical Listening

The ability to listen critically is essential in a democracy. On the job, in the community, at service clubs, in places of worship, in the family—there is practically no place you can go where critical listening is unimportant. Politicians, the media, salesmen, advocates of policies and procedures, and our own financial, emotional, intellectual, physical, and spiritual needs require us to place a premium on critical listening and the thinking that accompanies it.

The subject of critical listening deserves much more attention than we can afford it here. But there are three things to keep in mind. These three things were outlined by Aristotle, the classical Greek rhetorician, more than 2,000 years ago in his treatise, *The Rhetoric.* They are as follows: *ethos,* or speaker credibility; *logos,* or logical arguments; and *pathos,* or psychological appeals.

- ***Ethos:*** Credibility of the speaker is important. The two critical factors of speaker credibility are expertness and trustworthiness. A speaker may be expert or competent and still not be trustworthy. For example, an autocratic dictator of a certain third world country might be an expert on the question of his country's possession of nuclear arms; but his friend Giani would not trust him to tell him. On the other hand a person might be trustworthy, but not be an expert on the subject. Giani trusts his best friend; he would tell him the truth about nuclear arms in that third world country, if he knew and Giani asked him. But his information would be of questionable validity since he is simply not an expert in such things.

  When listening to a message that requires a critical judgment or response, ask yourself, "Is the speaker a credible source, one who is both an expert on the subject and one who can be trusted to be honest, unbiased, straight forward?" Remember that a person may have personality or charisma. But these do not take the place of credibility. A person may even be highly competent and an expert in one area and simply not be informed in another.

  An airforce officer is an expert on the use of airpower, and he is trustworthy. But you would not expect him to be an expert on buying used cars. He may be an expert on any or all of these things, but you would want to "check it out" before you plan to buy a used car.

  Effective critical listening requires careful judgment about the expertness and trustworthiness of the speaker. In fact, ethos or speaker's credibility may be the most important single factor in critical listening and thinking. However, ethos without logos is not enough.

- ***Logos:*** Even speakers with high ethos often make errors in logic, not by intention, but by accident, carelessness, inattention to detail, or lack of analysis. Critical listeners have a right to expect well supported arguments from speakers, arguments that contain both true propositions and valid inferences or conclusions.

When evaluating arguments, listeners should ask several questions about the proposition or statements made:

- Are the statements true?
- Are the data the best that can be obtained?
- Are the sources of the data known to the listeners? In other words do listeners know where the information came from?
- Is the data accurately portrayed?
- Is the data representative? That is, would all the data, or at least a preponderance of it show the same thing?

These questions may all be answered to your satisfaction, yet the logic may be faulty. For perhaps the data do not lead to or justify the inferences or conclusions drawn. Listeners should ask themselves the following questions:

- Is the conclusion a certainty or are exceptions possible?
- Were all cause-effect relationships established beyond doubt?
- Does the data justify the inference drawn or the conclusion given?
- Does the inference or conclusion "follow" from the data, or is there a *non sequitur*, which means literally, "it does not necessarily follow"?
- Is there evidence of strong logical thinking by the speaker?

Both ethos and logos are crucial elements of critical listening. But reliance on just these two elements without consideration of pathos would be akin to attempting to sit on a three-legged stool with one leg missing. Pathos is the third leg.

- ***Pathos:*** The psychological or emotional element of communication is often misunderstood and misused.

Simply said, speakers often use psychological appeals to gain an emotional response from listeners. Effective critical listeners carefully determine the focus of the speaker's message.

Speakers may appeal to any one or several needs, desires, or values that are important to us including: adventure, thrift, curiosity, fear, creativity, companionship, guilt, independence, loyalty, power, pride, sympathy, altruism. There are many others, of course; the list is a long one.

There are several questions critical listeners should ask themselves when assessing the pathos element:

- Is the speaker attempting to manipulate rather than persuade me?
- What is the speaker's intent?
- Is the speaker combining logos with pathos?
- Am I responding merely to the pathos?
- Next week or next year will I be satisfied with the decision I am making today?

Effective critical listening depends on the listener keeping all three elements of the message in the analysis and in perspective: ethos, or source credibility; logos, or logical argument; and pathos, or psychological appeals.

Discriminative Listening

The final type of listening is discriminative listening. It may be the most important type, for it is basic to the other four. By being sensitive to changes in the speaker's rate, volume, force, pitch, and emphasis, the informative listener can detect even nuances of difference in meaning. By sensing the impact of certain responses, such as "uh huh", or "I see", relationship listening can be strengthened. Detection of differences between sounds made by certain instruments in the orchestra, or parts sung by the a cappella vocal group, enhances appreciative listening. Finally, sensitivity to pauses, and other vocal and Non–verbal cues, allows critical listeners to more accurately judge not only the speaker's message, but his intentions as well.

Obviously, many people have good discriminatory listening ability in some areas but not in others. Little Venu has always been very adept at picking up minute differences in a person's voice that might signal feelings. She has a gift for discriminating and applying what she hears to relationship listening. But her ability to discriminate among the different sounds that come from an automobile engine is practically nil.

Although discriminative listening cuts across the other four types of listening, there are three things to consider about this type of listening.

- ***Hearing Ability:*** Obviously, people who lack the ability to hear well will have greater difficulty in discriminating among sounds. Often this problem is more acute for some frequencies, or pitches, than others. For example, a person may be less able to discriminate when the sound is coming from a bass voice than from a higher pitched one.
- ***Awareness of Sound Structure:*** Native speakers become quite proficient at recognizing vowel and consonant sounds that do or do not appear at the beginning, middle, or end of words. For example, a listener might hear "this sandal" when what the speaker said was "this handle"; but since English words do not begin with "sb", one would not mistake "this bean" for "this sbean".

  Attention to the sound structure of the language will lead to more proficient discriminatory listening. A person who pays attention to sound structure would recognize that a rapidly spoken "Idrankitfirst" could mean either "I drank it first" or "I'd rank it first". Recognition of the two meanings would cause the listener to seek clarification.
- ***Integration of Non–verbal Cues:*** The action, non-action, and vocal factors are important in understanding messages. Nowhere is attention to these factors more important than in effective discriminative listening. Words don't always communicate true feelings. The way

they are said, or the way the speaker acts, may be the key to understanding the true or intended meaning.

Effective listening, whether informative, relational, appreciative, critical, or discriminative, requires skill. In some cases, the skills are the same for the various types of listening; in some cases, they are quite different.

DEVELOPING LISTENING SKILLS

There are a number of situations when you need to solicit good information from others; these situations include interviewing candidates, solving work problems, seeking to help an employee on work performance, and finding out reasons for performance discrepancies.

Skill in communication involves a number of specific strengths. The first we will discuss involves listening skills. The following list suggests some for effective listening when confronted with a problem at work:

- Listen openly and with empathy to the other person.
- Judge the content, not the messenger or delivery; comprehend before you judge.
- Use multiple techniques to fully comprehend (ask, repeat, rephrase, etc.).
- Maintain active body state; fight distractions.
- Ask the other person for as much detail as he/she can provide; paraphrase what the other is saying to make sure you understand it and check for understanding.
- Respond in an interested way that shows you understand the problem and the employee's concern.
- Attend to non-verbal cues, body language, not just words; listen between the lines.
- Ask the other for his views or suggestions.
- State your position openly; be specific, not global.
- Communicate your feelings but don't act them out (e.g. tell a person that his behaviour really upsets you; don't get angry).
- Be descriptive, not evaluative; describe objectively, your reactions, consequences.

- Be validating, not invalidating ("You wouldn't understand"); acknowledge other's uniqueness, importance.
- Be conjunctive, not disjunctive (not "I want to discuss this regardless of what you want to discuss").
- Don't totally control conversation; acknowledge what was said.
- *Own up*: use "I", not "They"... not "I've heard you are non cooperative"
- Don't react to emotional words, but interpret their purpose.
- Practice supportive listening, not one way listening.
- Decide on specific follow-up actions and specific follow up dates.

A major source of problem in communication is defensiveness. Effective communicators are aware that defensiveness is a typical response in a work situation especially when negative information or criticism is involved. Be aware that defensiveness is common, particularly with subordinates when you are dealing with a problem. Try to make adjustments to compensate for the likely defensiveness. Realise that when people feel threatened they will try to protect themselves; this is natural. This defensiveness can take the form of aggression, anger, competitiveness, avoidance among other responses. A skillful listener is aware of the potential for defensiveness and makes needed adjustment. He or she is aware that self-protection is necessary and avoids making the other person spend energy defending the self.

In addition, a supportive and effective listener does the following:

- *Stops Talking*: Asks the other person for as much detail as he/she can provide; asks for other's views and suggestions.
- Looks at the person, listens openly and with empathy to the employee; is clear about his position; is patient.
- Listens and Responds in an interested way that shows

he/she understands the problem and the other's concern.

- Is validating, not invalidating ("You wouldn't understand"); acknowledges other's uniqueness, importance.
- Checks for understanding; paraphrases; asks questions for clarification.
- Doesn't control conversation; acknowledges what was said; let's the other finish before responding.
- Focuses on the problem, not the person; is descriptive and specific, not evaluative; focuses on content, not delivery or emotion.
- Attends to emotional as well as cognitive messages (e.g., anger); is aware of non-verbal cues, body language, etc.; listen between the lines.
- Reacts to the message, not the person, delivery or emotion.
- Makes sure he/she comprehends before he/she judge; asks questions.
- Uses many techniques to fully comprehend.
- Stays in an active body state to aid listening.
- Fights distractions.
- In a work situation, takes down notes; Decides on specific follow-up actions and specific follow up dates.

THE NEED FOR BETTER LISTENING

Listening is the neglected communication skill. While all of us have had instructions in reading, writing, and speaking, few have had any formal instruction in listening. This void in our education is especially interesting in light of research showing that most of us spend seven of every 10 minutes we are awake in some form of communication activity. Of these seven minutes (or 70 percent of the time we are awake), 10 percent is spent writing, 15 percent reading, 30 percent talking, and 45 percent listening.

Think of it! We spend nearly half of our communication time listening, but few of us make any real effort to be better listeners. For those who do, however, the effort pays great dividends: increased safety, higher productivity, faster learning, and better relationships.

Good listening is important to the Air Force—at times, absolutely crucial! Just how crucial is readily apparent from a report in a USAF air safety publication.* the report presents quotations from a taped conversation between a pilot and a control tower operator during routine landing preparations. The tower operator wants the aircraft to descend from 10 thousand feet to eight thousand feet. Here is that conversation.

Time	*Agency*	
1929:38	Approach Control:	"Turn right, heading 180. Descend and maintain eight thousand."
1929:42	Aircraft:	"Right 180 out of fifteen thousand for two thousand." (Aircraft's readback was interrupted by another aircraft and not acknowledged by approach control.)
1931:08	Aircraft:	"Steady 180 and passing ten thousand for two thousand."
1931:11	Approach Control:	"Roger."
1931:22	Approach Control:	"Your position 12 miles south-west of airport, maintain eight thousand feet."
1931:30	Aircraft:	"Roger, passing nine for two." (This transmission was not acknowledged by approach control.)
1933:05	Approach Control:	"Your position 19 miles south-west of airport. Turn right 200 for slight pattern extension."

The report goes on to say that radar and radio contact was lost "because both crewmen had uttered their final words to victims in a fatal accident of poor listening in the air and on the ground."

This avoidable accident is but one example in which listening played a crucial role. Effective listening is, in fact, crucial throughout the Air Force. Consider missile crew members who have the capability to unleash weapons of incredible destruction. The primary communication authorizing their launch is an encoded spoken transmission. Consider also command post, security police, and medical personnel who receive information primarily through the spoken word. A simple listening error in any of these areas could result in lost man-hours, equipment, or lives.

Now consider the fact that poor listening is costly in even the most routine staff communications and office operations. Directives to a staff or instructions to office personnel are often given only once. The greater the difference in rank between those giving the directives or instructions and those receiving them, the less inclined the receivers are to ask for clarification—lest they be considered dull, slow, or inattentive. It is important to listen carefully the first time.

Surveys show that Air Force managers put a premium on good listening. Strong listening skills consistently rank at or near the top of characteristics they desire in their subordinates. Nor are Air Force managers unique in this regard. Far from it—business organizations with a profit motive have long recognized the value of listening effectively. Chief executive officers and chief operating officers of companies large and small say that poor listening is the number one problem in their organizations. Furthermore, they declare that listening is the communication skill most crucial to success. Their comments provoke no surprise, since many formal studies have resulted in the same conclusions: Listening is crucial in the workplace.

But listening is also important in various places—in the house, at religious places, in civic clubs, and at social gatherings. In these and other places, listening to gain information may be less important than listening to improve relationships. Counsellors and other experts on interpersonal communication say that listening is the skill that can make or break a relationship. To a certain extent, this type of listening is important in the workplace as well; after all, we humans are relational individuals and it is sometimes as important to understand the person as what the person is saying. Even at work, then, there is a lot more to listening than just understanding the meaning of words.

There is no question but that listening is both crucial and neglected. It is therefore this book's purpose to help you develop better listening skills. The first step in becoming a better listener is to recognize certain false notions that many people hold about listening. Recognizing these fallacies will help you to avoid being trapped by them.

FALLACIES ABOUT LISTENING

Among the great hindrances to effective listening are the fallacies that people hold about listening. These false ideas often cause people to have inflated opinions of their own listening performance. Believing that they have no problem with listening, they make no effort to improve. Indeed, why should they? Not knowing that their listening skill is "broke," they see no need to "fix" it. Consequently, they don't take steps to improve. Knowing about these fallacies will assist you in avoiding this trap. Here, then, are several of the common ones.

Listening Is Not 'MY' Problem!

People generally believe they are better listeners than those around them. It is the people they work for, the ones who work with or for them, their family members, and their friends who have a problem in listening effectively—not them.

In a certain class or lead seminars on communication, participants were asked to assess themselves as listeners. With 10 being high and one being low, they were to rate themselves as listeners compared to the other members of the group. The average score was found to be about 7.5.

Next, they rated the other group members as listeners. That rating turned out to be 4.1 on average. In other words, they believed that listening is a problem, but that the problem belongs to someone else. Remember that each group member is being rated as part of the group by the others; that is, each member is part of the group receiving the 4.1 rating.

The point is simply this. The people around us believe that we have more of a problem listening effectively than they do.

This should tell us something. Listening is not just someone else's problem—it's ours.

Listening And Hearing Are The Same

Simply having good hearing does not make one a good listener. In fact, many people who have perfectly good hearing are not good listeners. Having good hearing does facilitate one's perception of sound; but good listeners don't simply hear words—they focus on the meaning. We communicate effectively with each other in so far as we share meaning.

If someone tells you something and you misunderstand him, effective communication has not occurred. If he tells you something and you understand what he meant—that is, if you two have an effective transfer or sharing of meaning—we say that the communication is effective. Effective listening implies that the listener understands what the speaker means.

The difference between hearing and listening can be stated this way: Hearing is the reception of sound, listening is the attachment of meaning to the sound. Hearing is passive, listening is active. Understanding the difference between hearing and listening is an important prerequisite for listening effectively.

Good Readers Are Good Listeners

This statement is often untrue, even though both reading and listening depend on the translation of words into meaning. Because of the shared translation function, there is obviously some kind of relationship between readings and listening; the problem is, many people mistakenly believe that all good readers are necessarily good listeners. Researchers who administer different standard reading tests to the same individual find a high positive correlation between the two sets of scores; that is, persons who score well on one reading test generally score well on another while persons who score low on one test tend to score low on another. Similar results are found by researchers who test individuals on standardized listening tests. Those who score high on one test tend to score high on another, and vice versa. Interestingly, however, there is often a surprisingly low correlation between one's scores on reading tests and that same person's scores on listening tests. For a demonstration of this result, consider the following experiment.

> A teacher divides a class into two sections, randomly assigning students until each section has half the students. Each new "class" is placed in a new, separate classroom. Each student in one class is given a short paper, told to read it once and then place it on the desk, blank side up. Students in the other class listen as the teacher delivers the paper as a speech. Students in both classes are then given identical tests on the material covered.

Experiments like this one consistently result in certain questions being answered correctly more often by those who read the paper while other questions are answered correctly more often by those who heard it delivered as a speech. This result is really not all that surprising. When we read a document, visual cues—margins, illustrations, punctuation—become factors. On the other hand, when we listen, the speaker's vocal emphasis, reading style, pauses, and the like influence our understanding. There is, then, a difference between processing information from the written word and processing it from the spoken word. The fact that some people are better at one than the other demonstrates the fallacy of believing that good readers are necessarily good listeners.

Incidentally, test results also show that most people score higher as readers than as listeners. Being a good reader is no guarantee that you are a good listener.

Smarter People Are Better Listeners

Obviously, intelligence plays a role in a person's capacity to listen. Persons with limited intelligence will be limited in their capacity to process the information contained in messages they receive. Conversely, those having high intelligence levels will possess a greater processing capacity. Yet, the belief that "smarter people are better listeners" is often false. In fact, evidence suggests that the reverse is often true.

Once a listening test and a standardized IQ test was administered to students in several college classes. The results of the listening test to the IQ scores for each student were compared. There was little correlation between listening test results and IQ scores—with one surprising exception: There was an inverse relationship between listening scores and IQ scores for those students having the very highest IQ scores. In other words, the smartest students actually scored lower on the listening test than did many students having lower IQ scores. These results lead to the conclusion that higher intelligence levels do not necessarily result in better listening among college students who possess the capacity—if not always the willingness—to listen. Further, higher intelligence may actually interfere with the listening of those who are the very smartest.

We must keep in mind that this study was conducted with a specific group—college students. Most were in their late teens and early twenties. And the test did not assess all types of listening. It required that students listen to conversations for two reasons: to gain information and to understand something about the speaker—what we can refer to as informative listening and relationship listening.

It is quite possible that the smarter students were bored with this test. If so, boredom could explain their lower performance. Whatever the reasons, however, the fact remains that smarter people are not necessarily better listeners.

Preoccupation

Sometimes we don't listen because we are preoccupied. We have so many things to think about. Our mind is full of ideas, facts, and worries. We are unable to put them aside while we listen. Nevertheless, good listening *demands* that we avoid preoccupation when someone is speaking to us.

Prejudice

Attitudes and feelings not tempered by logical thinking can lead to prejudice. Perhaps we don't like the speaker. Or the subject may be one that we know little about and "don't want to know."

May be we don't like the method of presentation. In any event, we are prejudiced against the presentation; we have prejudged it. Consequently, we may mentally argue with the speaker. Or we may simply "tune out." Prejudicial thinking can divert our attention away from what the speaker is saying.

Self-centeredness

Since we live with ourselves all day every day, most of us spend much more time thinking about ourselves than about others. It is therefore not surprising that self-concern interferes with our listening to what another is saying. We must work at transferring our concentration from "I" to "You"—from ourselves to the person doing the talking.

Stereotyping

As thinking and feeling human beings, we hold certain beliefs about a variety of subjects. We have "fixed" judgments or concepts which we believe to be true and correct. If a speaker presents evidence that contradicts our beliefs, we tend to ignore what is being said—either because it is not believable to us or because we don't want our ideas challenged. Good listeners do not allow themselves to be trapped by stereotypes.

Listening Skills Are Difficult To Learn

Actually, the skills themselves are not all that difficult—and initial progress is rapid. But learning to apply the skills consistently does take hard work. And becoming really proficient takes much time and practice—a lifetime to be exact. But the effort is definitely worthwhile.

THE PROCESS OF LISTENING

The first step in listening effectively is to recognize certain fallacies or false notions. The next step is to understand the process. Listening is a complex process—an integral part of the total communication process, albeit a part often ignored. This neglect results largely from two factors. First, speaking and writing (the sending parts of the communication process) are highly visible, and are more easily assessed than listening and reading (the receiving parts). And reading behaviour is assessed much more frequently than listening behaviour; that is, we are more often tested on what we read than on what we hear. And when we are tested on material presented in a lecture, generally the lecture has been supplemented by readings. Second, many of us aren't willing to improve our listening skills. Much of this unwillingness results from our incomplete understanding of the process—and understanding the process could help show us how to improve. To understand the listening process, we must first define it. Through the years, numerous definitions of listening have been proposed. Perhaps the most useful one defines listening as the process of receiving, attending, and understanding auditory messages; that is, messages transmitted through the medium of sound. Often, the steps of responding and remembering are also included.

The process moves through the first three steps—receiving, attending, understanding—in sequence. Responding and/or remembering may or may not follow. It may be desirable for the listener to respond immediately or to remember the message in order to respond at a later time. At times, of course, no response (at least no verbal response) is required. And the act of remembering may or may not be necessary. If someone tells you to "watch your step", you have no need to remember the message after you have completed that step.

Let's look at the parts—the three necessary ones and the two additional ones—one at a time. Consider the following analogy between the listening process and the electronic mail (E-mail) system. Suppose that you are the sender of a message and Mark the intended recipient.

Receiving

This step is easily understood. You may send a message to Mark by E-mail. It may be wonderfully composed and clear. You may have used effective techniques to organize and support your message. The subject may be one of great interest to Mark. Imagine further that he both admires and respects you, and that he likes to receive E-mail from you.

In short, you have done a good job and Mark wants to receive the message. But if he doesn't turn on his computer, he won't receive it. The message remains somewhere between your computer and his—between sender and receiver.

Much human listening fails for the same reason. Receivers simply are not connected or "tuned in" to the senders. Sometimes, the problem is a physiological one; for example, the receiver has a hearing deficiency due to a congenital or inherited weakness. Or perhaps the deficiency resulted from an accident, a disease, or prolonged exposure to loud noises. Sometimes the problem can be corrected through the use of mechanical devices that restore hearing loss, or through hearing aids that amplify sound. Scientists and engineers are constantly developing new products designed to correct and help specific types of hearing loss.

Remember that hearing and listening are not the same. Hearing is the reception of sound; listening is the attachment of meaning. Hearing is, however, a necessary prerequisite for listening and an important component of the listening process.

Attending

Let's continue with the E-mail analogy. When Mark turns his computer on, it will receive the message that you sent. But he must do more: he must attend to the message if the process is to continue. Perhaps he received a phone call just after he turned his computer on and had to move away from his desk; he does not know that you have sent a message. Or may be he didn't have an opportunity to read his E-mail that day.

Suppose that Mark is working on something else when the message arrives. His computer signals that he has mail from you. He wants to read it, but he decides that he will do it later. He continues to stay busy on another task, however, and forgets to read the message. Later, he may mistakenly "trash it" without ever reading it. Whatever the case, he doesn't attend to the message.

Human listening is often ineffective—or does not occur—for similar reasons. Receiving occurs, but attending does not. At any given time, numerous messages compete for our attention. The stimuli may be external, such as words spoken by a lecturer or printed on paper, or events occurring around us. Or the stimuli may be internal, such as a deadline we must meet tomorrow, a backache we developed by sitting too long at the computer, or the hunger pangs we experience because we didn't take time to eat lunch. Whatever the source of the stimuli, we simply can't focus on all of them at the same time. We therefore must choose, whether consciously or unconsciously, to attend to some stimuli and reject others. Three factors determine how these choices are made.

- ***Selectivity of attention:*** We direct attention to certain things to prevent an information overload. A common example makes the point. Suppose you are attempting to read a book and watch TV at the same time. Although some people claim they can do this, actually both activities suffer—and usually one more than the other. The material that is most engaging or interesting will attract your attention. At other times, something may interrupt or disturb your attention.

  One day as the principal was lecturing to a thousand students in an auditorium, a streaker dressed only in combat boots and a football helmet ran across the stage. Needless to say, the principal lost the attention of the audience. He tried for several minutes to regain their attention, then finally decided to dismiss the class 10 minutes early. He had always believed that he was a good lecturer and could hold the audience's attention, no matter what; he was wrong!

  Selectivity of attention explains why you "perk up" or pay attention when something familiar to you, such as your hometown or your favourite hobby, is mentioned. In fact, you may have been listening intently to a conversation when someone in a different conversation mentions your name. Immediately, the focus of your attention shifts to the conversation in which your name was mentioned.

- ***Strength of attention:*** Attention is not only selective; it possesses energy, or strength. Attention requires effort and desire. In the example of reading a book and watching TV, the receiver (reader/watcher) directed his or her primary attention toward either the book or the TV. Complete attention can be given to only one stimulus at a time, and necessary attention to only a limited number of stimuli at the same time.

If we spend too much energy on too many stimuli, we soon will not be paying attention to any of them. We are all familiar with aircraft accidents that were caused at least in part by controllers in the tower having to process too much information.

Consider also how we can be so attentive to a newspaper, a TV programme, a personal computer, a sports event, or another individual that we are oblivious to things around us. Watch a young couple in love sometime: You'll see a good example of intensity, or strength of attention.

Still another measure of attention strength is the length of time that the memory of something continues to influence us. At the age of 80 you may still remember vividly the baptism of your first grandchild, the first major league baseball game you attended, and the first time you kissed your wife—not necessarily in that order, of course. Strength of attention is important.

- ***Sustainment of attention:*** Just as attention is determined by selectivity and strength, it is affected by time of sustainment. Our attention wanes, and this fact is important to an understanding of listening.

  We can listen to some public speakers far longer than we can listen to others. Duration may depend on the subject, the setting, the way the speech is packaged, and on the speaker's delivery. But no matter how articulate and skilled the speaker, or how interesting the content, our attention finally ends. If for no other reason, the human body requires sleep or attention to other bodily needs, the mind can only pay attention for as long as the body can sit still.

Selectivity, strength, and sustainment determine attention. Receiving and attending are prerequisites to the rest of the listening process. The third step in that process is understanding.

Understanding

Someone has said, "Communication begins with understanding." How true! A message may have been sent and received, and the receiver may have attended to the message—yet, there has been no effective communication. Effective communication depends on understanding; that is, effective communication does not take place until the receiver *understands* the message. Understanding must result for communication to be effective.

Let's return to the E-mail analogy. Suppose Mark received the E-mail message, "opened" it, and read it. Has effective communication occurred? Not necessarily. Even though he read every word of your message, he may not have understood what you meant.

There are several possible reasons for the misunderstanding. Perhaps he expected the message to say something that it didn't say; his understanding of it may therefore be more in line with his own expectations than what it actually said. We often hear or read what we expect rather than what was actually said or written.

Or perhaps the real point of the message was "tucked away", obscured by several other tidbits of information. And he missed the point. In listening, the key point is sometimes missed. A worker may tell a supervisor several things that happened while the supervisor was out of the office. While relating all the events, the worker mentions that the boss asked that the supervisor call upon his return.

The supervisor missed this important piece of information because he was not "ready" for it; that is, he was trying to understand the other parts of the message. Later, he asks the worker why he had failed to tell him that his boss wanted to see him. But the worker *had* told him; he just didn't understand.

Our expectations and/or our failure to get the point often lead to misunderstanding. But the major reason for Mark not understanding the E-mail he received from you was probably something else: the words you used and the manner in which you arranged them. Neither of you was necessarily "at fault"; you too simply attached different meanings to the words. You attached one meaning to those words, he attached another. Both of you communicate effectively with each other only in so far as you share meanings for the symbols—verbal or non–verbal—that you are using.

With E-mail, the message is limited to words or other visual symbols that represent words. In listening, both verbal and Non–verbal symbols are crucial to understanding. Consider the roles they play.

VERBAL SYMBOLS

Verbal communication means communicating through the use of words, whether spoken or written. Two barriers obstruct our understanding of verbal communication.

Barrier #1: The same words mean different things to different people. This barrier is a common one, and it may be experienced whenever any two people attempt to communicate.

You may tell your colleague that the temperature in the office is quite comfortable. Your "quite comfortable", however, is her "uncomfortable": 20°C is comfortable for you; 25°C is comfortable for her. The same word can mean different things to different people.

A friend tells you he will be over in five minutes. To him, five minutes means "soon"—perhaps any time in the next half hour. For you, on the other hand, attach a literal meaning: Five minutes means five minutes.

The same words having different meanings for different people caused only minor irritation.

The fire inspector said that workers exhibit great caution when they are working around gasoline drums. They take great care not to smoke or ignite matches nearby. But when the drums are emptied, and labeled "empty gasoline drums", caution is thrown to the wind. Workers feel comfortable in striking matches and smoking cigarettes in the area. Ironically, vapours that emanate from "empty" drums are much more volatile than liquid gasoline.

The word "empty" holds a different meaning for the workers than for the experienced fire inspector, who knows that the potential for disaster is present. The next example shows how a misunderstanding of one word's meaning can lead to tragic consequences.

One night, after sunset, a traveller stopped at a convenience store to ask directions. The man behind the counter pointed to a traffic signal a block away and said, "Go to that intersection, take an immediate left, go about a mile. It will be the big red building on your right."

The traveller repeated, "Go to the traffic light, take an immediate left, go a mile to the red building on my right. Is that it?"

"That's right," said the convenience store operator.

Unfortunately, the traffic light was on the corner heading into the intersection and the man in the store had neglected to mention the grassy median that separated northbound and southbound lanes. The traveller took an "immediate left" and headed south in the northbound lane. Less than half mile later, he found himself on the edge of an unattended swampy area. Only thanks for his brakes!.

When the same words mean different things to different people, misunderstanding occurs.

- ***Barrier #2:*** Different words sometimes mean the same thing. Many things are called by more than one name.

For example, when Dolly and her adolescent son, Sidh, went to a restaurant in the South UK shortly after they had moved there from the Midwest, Sidh asked the waiter to bring him a "pop". The waiter didn't understand until Sidh said, "You know—pop, it comes in a bottle or a can; you shake it and it fizzes". The waiter said, "Oh! You mean a soda". But "soda" meant quite something else to Sidh, and there were a few more moments of confusion until the waiter and Sidh understood one another.

Soft drink, soda, and pop all mean the same thing when used in the same context. The name used depends on who is doing the talking. How many things in the English language are called by more than one name? For a starter, consider that the 500 most commonly used words in our language have a total of about 15,000 definitions—an average of 30 per word.

Our language is marked by its multiusage. If you doubt it, describe some object or animal in detail to several talented artists and ask them to draw what you describe. Chances are that each one will draw a distinctively different picture.

These two barriers—same words meaning different things and different words meaning the same thing—can be overcome if you realise the following fact: *Meanings are not in words, meanings are in people.* We listen more effectively when we consider the message in relation to its source. Good listeners always consider who the sender of the message is. Knowing something about the sender pays big dividends when it comes to understanding the message.

NON–VERBAL SYMBOLS

We use non–verbal symbols to transmit many times more information than our verbal symbols carry. We communicate non–verbally through action factors, non action factors, and vocal factors. Each suggests a barrier to listening.

Misinterpretation Of The Action

Eye contact, gestures, and facial expression are action factors that affect the meaning we attach to a message. For that matter, any movement or action carries meaning. When someone walks quickly away from a conversation or taps a pencil on the desk during a conversation, we may conclude that the person is in a hurry or is bored. Our conclusions may or may not be correct, however. We may conclude that speakers who twitch, or otherwise seem to us unsure, are nervous when, in fact, they may not be.

Misinterpretation Of Non-Action Symbols

The clothes you wear, the automobile you drive, and the objects in your office—all these things communicate something about you. In addition, your respect of someone else's needs for time and space affects how he interprets your messages. If you are to see him at noon but arrive 15 minutes late, your tardiness may affect how he interprets what you say to him. Or if you "crowd" him—get "too close" to him emotionally—when speaking, he may "tune you out"; that is, he may "hear" but not "listen to" your message.

Misinterpretation Of The Voice

The quality, intelligibility, and variety of the voice affect the listener's understanding. Quality refers to the overall impression the voice makes on others. Listeners often infer from the voice whether the speaker is happy or sad, fearful or confident, excited or bored. Intelligibility (or understandability) depends on such things as articulation, pronunciation, and grammatical correctness. But variety is the spice of speaking. Variations in rate, volume, force, pitch, and emphasis are some of the factors that influence our understanding of the speaker's message. Receiving, attending and understanding are all crucial if effective listening is to occur, for communication can accurately be defined as the sharing or understanding of meaning. Often, however, the steps of responding and remembering are part of the listening process. Responding and remembering are indicators of listening accuracy.

RESPONDING

The listening process may end with understanding, since effective communication and effective listening may be defined as the accurate sharing or understanding of meaning. But a response may be needed—or at least helpful. And there are different types of responses.

Direct Verbal Responses

These may be spoken or written. Let's continue with the E-mail analogy. After Mark has received, attended to, and understood the message you sent, he may respond verbally. If your message asked a question or sought his coordination, he might type a response on Mark's computer and reply to you. Perhaps you requested that he call you or come to see you, in which case he do so. Or you might have asked him to write a position paper or think about an issue and give you some advice, in which case he might send a quick E-mail response indicating that he will get back to you later.

Responses That Seek Clarification

Mark may use E-mail to ask for additional information, or he may talk to you either on the telephone or face-to-face. He may be very direct in my request, or he may just say, "tell me more about it".

Responses That Paraphrase

Mark may say something like, "in other words, what you are saying is...." A paraphrase gives the sender a chance to agree, or to provide information to clarify the message.

Non–verbal Responses

Many times, a non–verbal response is all that is needed; indeed, it may even be the preferred type of response. The knowing nod of the head, an understanding smile, or a "thumbs up" may communicate that the message is understood.

Responding, then, is a form of feedback that completes the communication transaction. It lets the sender know that the message was received, attended to, and understood.

REMEMBERING

Memorization of facts is not the key to good listening. Yet memory is often a necessary and integral part of the listening process. Some would go so far as to say, "if you can't remember it, you weren't listening."

This statement is often untrue. Think for example, of the times you heard a good joke but can't remember it long enough to get home and tell it; or the number of times you have gone to the grocery store and couldn't remember what you were asked to buy. And the most frustrating situation of all—you were introduced to someone and can't recall the name five minutes later. We often say, "I can remember faces, but I can't remember names." At times, something will "jog" our memory, such as hearing another joke, seeing a similar product on the grocery store shelf, or meeting someone else with the same first name.

What is the relationship between memory and listening? Understanding the differences between short-term memory and long-term memory will help explain the relationship.

Short–Term Memory

With short-term memory, information is used immediately—within a few seconds, for example, as with a phone number that we look up. Short-term memory has a rapid forgetting rate and is very susceptible to interruption. And the amount of information that can be retained is quite limited, though it varies somewhat with variations in the material to be retained. For example, most of us can remember only very few random numbers (4, 13, 9, 53, 274, 6, 491, 713, 2810, 1, 7555, 111). But if there is a pattern (1, 2, 4, 8, 16, 32, 64, 128, 256, 512, 1024, 2048), the task is much easier.

Long–Term Memory

Long-term memory allows us to recall information and events hours, days, weeks—even years—later. You remember, for example, things that happened to you when you were growing up, songs you learned, people you knew. You may have been unaware of those memories for long periods of time, and then the right stimulus caused you to recall them. Perhaps the aroma of a freshly baked pie called to mind your grandmother, who used to make great apple pies years ago.

□□

Chapter 6

Components of Effective Listening

While there are many ways to construct a list of practical suggestions on how to be a better listener, we will consider them in terms of what works best in three major categories:

- What you *think* about listening?
- What you *feel* about listening?
- What you *do* about listening?

You can learn to listen effectively; look now at the components of that learning: thinking, feeling, doing.

WHAT YOU *THINK* ABOUT LISTENING?

Although thinking, feeling, and doing go hand in hand, the thinking (or cognitive) domain of learning is perhaps the best place to begin. After all, effective listening takes effort—it requires maximum thinking power. Here are six suggestions.

Understand The Complexities Of Listening

Most of us take good listening for granted. Therefore, we don't work very hard at improving. But listening is a complex activity, and its complexity explains the emphasis given earlier in the book to understanding the fallacies, processes, and types of listening.

Knowing the fallacies about listening can keep you from being trapped by them. Knowing that the process involves more than just receiving messages will help you focus on not just receiving, but the other components as well. Recognizing the five major types of listening will help you to consciously direct your energies toward the type of listening required for the circumstance of the moment.

Listening requires an active response, not a passive one. Effective listening doesn't just happen; it takes thought—and thinking can be hard work. But there is no other way to become an effective listener. Think about the complexities of listening, and work to understand them.

Prepare To Listen

Preparation consists of three phases—long-term, mid-term, and short-term. We said earlier that becoming an effective listener is a lifetime endeavor; in other words, expanding your listening ability will be an ongoing task. But there are two things you can do to improve your listening skills for the long term:

- Practice listening to difficult material
- Build your vocabulary.

Too many people simply do not challenge their listening ability. Since most of today's radio and television programmes do not require concentrated or careful listening, your listening skills do not improve through continued exposure to them. And you have to stretch if you want to grow. Force yourself to listen carefully to congressional debates, lectures, sermons, or other material that requires concentration.

Building your vocabulary will improve your conversational skills and your reading skills as well as your listening skills. And the more words you learn, the better listener you will become.

Mid-term preparation for listening requires that you do the necessary background study before the listening begins. Background papers, prebriefs, and an advance look at a hard copy of briefing slides or charts will assist you in being ready to listen.

Short-term preparation may be defined as an immediate readiness to listen. When the speaker's mouth opens, you should open your ears. That is not the time to be hunting for a pen, reading a letter from home, or thinking about some unrelated subject. Good listeners—really good listeners—are in the "spring-loaded position to listen". It is important to *prepare* to listen.

Adjust To The Situation

No listening situation is exactly the same as another. The time, the speaker, the message—all change. But many other variables also affect listening, though less obviously so: physiological variables such as rest, hunger, comfort, endurance; psychological variables such as emotional stability, rapport with the speaker, knowledge of the subject; and physical factors such as size and colour of the room. Obviously, some of these things will have a positive effect on your listening while others will have a negative effect.

A thick foreign accent, poor grammar, a room with poor acoustics, and the subject of the previous speaker—all may present special barriers to effective listening. However, being aware of the barriers and thinking about how to overcome them can help you improve the situation.

Good listeners are never trapped into thinking that any communication transaction or listening situation is exactly like any other. The Grecian philosopher Heraclitus said it well: "You can't step into the same stream twice". Things change. By thinking about the unique factors of the situation, you can do your most effective job as a listener. Adjust to the situation!

Focus On Ideas Or Key Points

At times, you may understand the process, you may have prepared well, and you may be able to adjust to the situation—yet you fail as a listener. This failure results because you didn't listen to the right things. For example, you may remember a funny story the speaker told to make a point; but you missed the point.

Others boast, "I listen only for the facts". By concentrating exclusively on individual supporting facts, they may actually miss the main ideas. Facts A, B, and C may be interesting in their own right, but the speaker's reason for offering them is usually to develop a generalization from them. Generalizations, not facts, are usually most important.

In studies conducted some years ago at the University of New Mexico, it was discovered that students who did best on all but rote memory examinations were those who listened for key points and ideas. Interestingly, those who attempted to memorize minute details did only slightly better on low-level rote memory exams than the individuals who focused on ideas—and they did much worse when long-term retention was the criterion. While there are some exceptions, as when listening for directions to someone's house or memorizing a mathematical formula, it is usually best to focus on ideas or key points.

Capitalize On The Speed Differential

Thought can operate much faster than speech. An average person may speak two or three words a second—120 to 180 words a minute. In bursts of enthusiasm, we may even speak a little faster. Most public speakers speak somewhat slower, especially to large audiences. Yet most listeners can process up to 500 words per minute, depending on the nature and difficulty of the material.

A machine that compresses speech on tape, but without the distortions is normally associated with fast forwarding a tape or simply playing a tape or record at a faster speed. Compression is accomplished through systematic removal of small segments—so small that distortion is not noticed by listeners.

Experiments in which listening time is cut in half—an hour lecture is listened to in half the time—reveal little, if any, significant loss in listening and learning. Admittedly, listeners are ready for a break because there is no time for their minds to wander. Effective listening requires hard thinking, especially if the material is challenging.

The results of these experiments point to the possibility of capitalizing on the speed differential. Unfortunately, the differential between speed of thought and speed of speech promotes daydreaming or concentrating on something other than what is being said. This is not the case with good listeners, however; they use the time differential to good advantage. They summarize, anticipate, and formulate questions based on the speaker's message.

Organize Material For Learning

Obviously, speakers can enhance listening through careful organization and presentation of ideas. And if questions are appropriate, you can seek clarification of any points you fail to understand. Often, however, questioning is not permitted or, perhaps due to time constraints or the size of the audience, is inappropriate. What can you do?

Remembering that the speed differential exists, you can arrange the material in your mind or in your notes as it's being presented. This will help you understand and remember it later. You can prepare yourself to retain the information to be presented by asking these questions: What point is the speaker trying to make? What main ideas should I remember? How does this information relate to what I already know?

Reorganizing the material you need to learn, and seeking relationships between the new material and what you already know, requires concentrated thinking. It is easier to simply "tune out". There must have been a time in your early college years when you could not see the relevance of some required classes to your course of study. But someday you came to understand that all information was part of a large mosaic or universe of knowledge. When that happened, you valued all learning. Always look for how the information relates to what you already know and what you need to know, and you will always find something.

WHAT YOU *FEEL* ABOUT LISTENING?

We began by discussing what you think about listening because effective listening requires rigorous cognitive processing, or thought. But possession of the sharpest mind will not make you a good listener if your feelings are wrong. In other words, what you feel about listening is important. Here are six suggestions for improving your "feel" for listening.

Want To Listen

This suggestion is basic to all others, for it simply says that you must have intent to listen. We can all recall having been forced to listen to a speech or a briefing that we didn't really want to listen to. And listening under duress seldom results in understanding or enjoyment, although there are exceptions. Perhaps you have attended a meeting or a social event out of a sense of duty, yet found it to have been profitable. The reason? Probably, since you were there, you decided to make the best of the situation; that is, you made up your mind to listen. Sometimes you don't want to listen. At other times, your actions may indicate that you don't want to listen when you really do. And at still other times, you may be unaware that you don't want to listen. All three of these situations are affective or attitudinal; that is, they involve your feelings about listening.

Individuals may often stop by your office and ask if they can talk for a few minutes. Perhaps they are seeking advice, telling about a project, or seeking clarification on a directive. Whatever the case, if you are not meeting with someone else or working against a deadline, you invite them in. But you must honestly admit that your mind sometimes wanders and you find yourself looking at phone messages, fiddling with a paper clip, or looking at your guest with a blank stare. The visitor usually becomes uneasy, hurries the discussion, and offers to come back another time. You pretend that you are really listening, but your actions betray you. It is difficult—indeed, nearly impossible—to really listen if you don't have a mind to. You must *want* to listen.

Delay Judgment

There are times when you must be a critical or judgmental listener. You must weigh the merits of what the speaker is saying. At times, you must make crucial decisions based on what you hear. There are also times when you must judge the speaker. Job interviews, campaign promises, speech contests—all are examples of where judgment of the speaker is important. The problem is, though, that you may be judgmental when you shouldn't be. You may judge the speaker instead of the content, or you may form judgments before the speaker has finished.

A boy who was one month shy of being 16 decided to confess to his father that he had driven the family car on the previous night. His younger sister's promised ride to dramatics class hadn't arrived, and it was the night of her final rehearsal before a performance. So he made the decision to take her even though he did not yet have a driver's license. He was also quite sure that he hadn't been seen and would never be found out. Still, his conscience was bothering him and his family had stressed honesty and openness. He decided to tell his father. Upon hearing that the boy had taken the car, his father became furious. He scarcely heard the reason, and he failed to consider that the boy had taken it upon himself to confess. He told the boy that the act would delay his getting a driver's license. Then the father rethought the situation and said, "Son, I acted hastily. My emotions got the best of me. You were wrong to drive the car because you broke the law. But, frankly, I am proud of you for three reasons: you got your sister to dramatics rehearsal, you were honest about it, and you are my son."

Delaying judgment and judging the content rather than the speaker will lead to better listening and more honest communication.

Admit Your Biases

Let's face it: Everyone is human! We all have likes and dislikes; some things turn us on, others turn us off. These characteristics are natural and to be expected. The problem comes when we let our biases—our likes and dislikes—get in the way of understanding the speaker's message.

Suppose you have had three bad experiences with people from Mumbai and you learn that the speaker you have come to hear is from Mumbai, you may have a tendency to immediately distrust him, or to discredit whatever he has to say. Only by admitting your prejudice against people from Mumbai will you be able to think beyond your past experience and listen effectively to what this speaker has to say.

Before you reject the example as irrelevant, consider a time in your past when you got sick after eating a certain food. You knew the sickness was caused by a virus and not the food, but it was quite a while before that food again tasted good to you. In a similar way, bias from past experience can influence what you hear and the meaning you derive from it. If you want to be an effective listener, you must know and admit your biases.

Don't Tune Out "Dry" Subjects

Whenever you are tempted to "tune out" something because you think it will be boring or useless, remember that you cannot evaluate the importance of the message until you have heard it. By then, it is probably too late to ask the speaker to repeat everything that was said; the opportunity to listen effectively will have passed.

As was stated earlier, you must *intend* to listen. Effective listeners have discovered the value of listening to messages they might have initially considered to be "dry". Sometimes the messages aren't so dry after all. And even when they are, there still may be something of value in them.

Accept Responsibility For Understanding

Don't assume this attitude: "Here I am! Teach me—if you can". Such listeners believe knowledge can be poured into them as water is poured into a jug. And they believe the responsibility rests with the one doing the pouring; that is, they believe it is the speaker's fault if effective listening does not occur.

Encourage Others To Talk

This point applies to those situations in which you find yourself "one-on-one", in a small group discussion, or any other setting that requires exchanges of vocal communication. But you can't listen if no one is talking.

WHAT YOU *DO* ABOUT LISTENING?

What we think about listening and what we feel about listening are both fundamental to skillful listening. But the skills themselves are *crucial*. Skills form the psychomotor—the "doing"—element of listening. Here are six crucial skills.

Establish Eye Contact With The Speaker

Studies show that listening has a positive relationship with eye contact. In other words, the better eye contact you have with the speaker, the better you will listen. And while eye contact is especially important in relationship listening, it is also important for the other kinds of listening: informative, appreciative, critical, and discriminative. A final point deserves discussion: Never sleep when someone is talking to you! This point may seem self-evident. But let's face it—in the "busyness" of our lives, we tend to become passive whenever we listen. Passivity promotes reduced attention, which in turn allows drowsiness to occur. In most cases, it is better to stand up, or even to leave the room, rather than fall asleep.

Take Notes Effectively

Some people recommend that you not take notes so you can focus your attention wholly on what the speaker is saying. This practice works well for listeners who are blessed with a great memory; most of us aren't. Taking notes will not only help you remember, it will help you organize what the speaker is saying. And it may even aid your understanding and retention—after all, effective note taking will require you to think.

Be A Physically Involved Listener

Just what does this statement mean? As you have already seen, listening requires more than just hearing. You have also seen that making eye contact and taking notes will help to keep you from becoming passive. But there is more: Active listening takes energy and involvement.

Avoid Negative Mannerisms

Everyone has mannerisms. Watch anyone for a period of time and you will be convinced of this fact. If your mannerisms do not cause a negative reaction, don't worry about them. If a mannerism is positive or encouraging and brings a positive response, make a mental note to do it more often. Unfortunately, some mannerisms are negative or distracting. These should be avoided. In short, any mannerism or behaviour that detracts from the speaker or the message should be avoided. Such things hinder the speaker, divert the attention of other listeners, and prevent you from being the best listener you can be.

Exercise Your Listening Muscles

Actually, there are no muscles technically involved with listening—but this thought reminds us that listening takes practice. Just as an athlete must work out regularly and a musician must practice daily, so you must work consistently to be an effective listener. But consistent practice in itself is not enough. The difficulty of the message is also important. Exposure to challenging material and difficult listening situations will stretch your ability and build your listening muscles.

Suppose you knew that you would be required to carry a 50-kg weight fifty meters in less than a minute. You wouldn't practice by carrying a 30-kg weight. You would practice by carrying at least a 50-kg weight, and you probably would condition yourself to carry it more than hundred meters in less than a minute.

With this kind of practice, you would be more than equal to the task. And so it is with listening: Practice to *at least* the level you will be required to perform—perhaps a bit.

Finally, "s-t-r-e-t-c-h" your vocabulary. We've said this before, but nothing will pay greater listening dividends. Learn the meanings of new words and acronyms. Listen to and read material that contains challenging words. Keep a dictionary nearby. Look up new words as you read them, or jot them down as you listen so you can look up the meanings later.

Follow The Golden Rule

Do unto others as yo u would have them do unto you. The central focus of all effective communication is "other directedness". There are exceptions to most other listening rules.

There are times when a listener shouldn't prepare; preparation may prevent openness to new ideas. There are times when the objective is not to focus on key points, but to listen for subordinate ideas or supporting material. There are times when we should not delay judgment—we must act! But while these and other rules have exceptions, not so for the Golden Rule. The effective listener is *always* directed, focused on the other person. Be the kind of listener you want others to be when you are talking. Ask "How would I want others to listen to me?" That's how to be an effective listener.

□□

Chapter 7

Speaking and Speech Improvement

For one to develop good public speaking abilities, speaking skills have to be learned, practiced and evaluated over a period of time. The first rule of thumb to be able to speak effectively is planning what to say. What is the main idea of what you are trying to convey? Organize your thoughts so they lead to the main idea of the message you are trying to send across. Once you have arrived at your main idea, take a short brief and ask your audience if they are following you. By doing so, you know if you are off tangent on what you are saying or still on the right path. Ask your listeners if they understood what you were saying so that you are both on the right page. Make sure you keep your conversation focused and direct to the point.

Another point, when developing your communication skills, is to take note of the style you use when speaking and expressing yourself. The speaking style you use has a large impact on the audience you are speaking to especially if you want to be convincing. When speaking, strive to be warm and enthusiastic. Doing this, your audience will be responsive and perfect interaction can be formed. It is normal to expect questions during a conversation and always be prepared to answer them. When answering, take your time by paraphrasing the question to be sure you are certain of what it means. In situations where you do not know the answer to the question, do not make up an answer, instead, say you do not know the answer.

PREPARING TO TALK

Recent studies show that speaking in front of a group is by far the greatest fear of most people. It ranks ahead of the fear of dying, riding in an airplane, or failure in other areas of one's personal life. Unless you are highly unusual, at some time in your life you have talked to a group of people and your knees began shaking, your voice quivered, your head ached, and the only dry place on your body was the inside of your mouth. Then the strange muscle spasms began. One eyelid began to twitch uncontrollably. Your legs felt like soft rubber. And then it happened: Your memory, on its own and for no apparent reason, left you. At this point you promised yourself that you would never get yourself in this situation again.

Although the fear of speaking is common, studies show that one of the most admired qualities in others is their ability to speak in front of a group. Furthermore, other things being equal, the person who can communicate ideas clearly will be more successful. The remainder of this book is directed toward helping you be the kind of speaker others admire—the kind who gets the job done in every speaking situation.

TYPES OF SPEAKING

There are several types of speaking patterns. Although most of the same general principles and techniques apply to all types, there are some differences.

Briefing

The best briefings are concise and factual. Their major purpose is to inform—tell about a concept, operation, or mission. At times they also direct—enable listeners to perform a procedure or carry out instructions. At other times they advocate or persuade—support a certain solution and lead listeners to accept that solution.

Every good briefing has the virtues of accuracy, brevity, and clarity. These are the ABCs of the briefing. Accuracy and clarity characterize all good speaking, but brevity distinguishes the briefing from other types of speaking. By definition, a briefing is brief, concise, and direct.

Teaching Lecture

The lecture is the method of instruction most often used. As the name implies, the primary purpose of a teaching lecture is to teach or to inform students about a given subject. For convenience, teaching lectures can be divided into the following types:

- Formal lectures, where the communication is generally one-sided with no verbal participation by the students.
- Informal lectures, usually presented to smaller audiences and allowing for verbal interaction between the instructor and students.

Speech

A speech generally has one of three basic purposes: to inform, to persuade, or to entertain. The *informative speech* is a narration concerning a specific topic but does not involve a sustained effort to teach. Speeches to civic clubs, orientation talks, and presentations at commanders' calls are examples of speeches to inform.

The *persuasive speech* is designed to move an audience to belief or action on some topic, product, or other matter. Recruiting speeches to high school graduating classes, budget defences and courts-martial summations are all primarily speeches to persuade. The *entertaining speech* gives enjoyment to the audience. The speaker often relies on humour and vivid language as a primary means of entertaining the listeners. A speech at a dining-out may be a speech to entertain.

AUDIENCE

Talking to hear one's own voice may feed the ego and even cause self-persuasion, but whatever type of speaking you are doing; the goal should be to communicate with others. A basic assumption, then, is that all speaking should be audience-centered. Since speakers have a primary responsibility of adapting the message to the audiences, they need to know as much about their audiences as possible.

Audience Analysis

There are two reliable methods for gaining information about audiences. Used together they can be extremely useful.

- The first is to organize information you already have about the audience. Knowing such variables as age, sex, rank, and experience can help you relate to the audience. If one or more of these or similar variables separates you from the audience, you may want to give special attention to ways of emphasizing similarities and reducing differences.
- The second method, when you have not talked to a particular group before, is to check with someone who has. Perhaps a friend or colleague has already talked to the same group and can tell you what to expect. It is better to know about audience behaviour before one speaks.

Audience Attitude

In some instances, you may have to face a hostile audience. An extreme example of a speaker facing a hostile audience is when the President must confront a group of militants on the official lawn. In such circumstances, the emotions of the audience are so great that effective communication becomes very difficult.

Most likely you will never have to speak to an overly hostile audience, but you may have to speak to one that is mildly hostile either to you or to your ideas. What can you do? Assuming that you are determined to be heard and the audience is willing to give you a chance, hostility can often be overcome. Clearly, your first task as a speaker is to change the audience attitude—if not to friendliness, then at least to a more neutral position. Your chances for success are much greater if you somehow build rapport with your listeners. Often this can be done by using one or more of the following techniques:

- Avoid behaving in a conceited or antagonistic manner.
- Demonstrate a genuine concern for your listeners.
- Exhibit friendliness and warmth toward your listeners.
- Emphasize similarities between your listeners and you.
- Be honest and straightforward.
- Use humour that is in good taste, especially if it is at your own expense.

- Indicate your association with people who are held in high esteem by the audience.
- Do not let negative, Non–verbal aspects of your behaviour contradict what you are saying.
- Demonstrate that you are an expert and have done your homework on the subject.
- Refrain from stating the main idea or conclusion at the outset. Present your facts first that you and your listeners agree upon, and then build toward your conclusion.

Most audiences will be friendly. They consist of people who are, for the most part, favourably disposed toward you as a speaker. Most people want you to do a good job. Furthermore, they usually are not in violent disagreement with your point of view. An informative briefing to other members of your organization, a speech to a local civic club, and a teaching lecture in the classroom are examples of speaking before friendly audiences.

SUBJECT

You will seldom have to look around for something to talk about. The subjects are implicit in the work of the organization. A staff briefing, for example, arises from the need to communicate certain subject matter. A teaching lecture is given to satisfy a particular curriculum need. On the other hand, a formal speech to persuade, inform, or entertain may provide you with more latitude in selecting the subject.

Selecting The Subject

On some occasions, the subject of your speech will be determined—at least partly—by the group. A local civic club, for instance, may ask you to talk to them about a job, hobby, or community project you are heading up. At other times. the choice of the subject will be left entirely up to you. Almost always, however, you will be free to choose the particular aspect or area of your subject that you wish to emphasize. There are several questions you can ask yourself about the subject or aspect of the subject you choose to talk about:

- Is this the best subject I can think of? Certainly this is a tough question. But you can answer it more wisely if you consider a number of subjects. As a rule, a carefully selected subject or aspect of the subject chosen after some thought will be a better choice than the "straw-clutching" effect that characterizes many searches for suitable subjects.
- Is this a subject that I already know something about and can find more? If not, then perhaps you should search elsewhere. There is no substitute for complete and authoritative knowledge of the subject.
- Am I interested in the subject? If you are not interested in what you will be talking about, you will find preparation a dull task, and you will have difficulty in capturing the interest of the audience. Talking about a community service project on which you have spent many hours or a new programme that you have helped implement on the job is probably much closer to your heart than a subject that you found while searching through a list of suggested topics.
- Is the subject suitable for my audience? Does it fit their intellectual capacity? Is it a subject that they will be interested in? A subject may be suitable or interesting to an audience if it vitally concerns their well-being, offers solutions to a problem they have, is new or timely, or if there is a conflict of opinion about it.
- Can the subject or aspect of the subject be discussed adequately in the time I have? One of the greatest problems many speakers have is that they fail to narrow their subject. Because of this problem, they generally do one of two things:
  - They don't adequately cover the subject, or
  - They talk too long. Both results are bad.

Narrowing The Subject

Some subjects are so broad or complex that you cannot possibly do justice to them in a single speech. In ten minutes you cannot tell much about "Reliance Industry", but perhaps you can adequately cover "The Reliance Retail". Speakers often tackle subjects that are too broad. You can pare a big topic down to size by moving from the general to the specific. The general and abstract topic may be successfully narrowed to the more concrete and specific.

Limit your subject in terms of your own interests and qualifications, your listeners' needs and demands, and the time allotted to your speech.

Choosing A Title

The title is a specific label given to the speech—an advertising slogan or catchword that catches the spirit of the speech and tantalizes the potential audience. Generally, the exact phrasing of the title is not decided until the speech has been built. At other times it may come to mind as you work on the speech. At still other times it may come early and guide your planning. An effective title should be relevant, provocative, and brief.

Listeners do not like to be misled. If the speech has to do with communication, then some reference to communication should be in the title. On the other hand, don't include words in the title merely to get attention if they have no relevance to the speech itself. "The Eleventh Commandment" is a relevant title for a speech that addresses the fact that the commandment of "Thou shall not get caught" has seemed to replace some of the other commandments. "A Pat on the Back, A Punch in the Mouth" is certainly a more provocative title than "How Positive and Negative Reinforcement Affects Our Children". "You Cannot Not Communicate" is briefer and more provocative than "The Impossibility of Failing to Communicate."

Although the preceding three titles are all rather catchy, sometimes the direct approach is very effective". A speech or lecture on effective listening might simply be titled "Effective Listening". Both of these titles are relevant, provocative (due to the subject matter itself), and brief.

Objectives

The purposes for speaking—informative, persuasive, entertaining—are important. But the general responses and specific responses you expect from the talks you give are also significant.

- *General Responses:* The purposes of speaking suggest the general kinds of responses desired from the audience. An informative presentation seeks audience understanding. A persuasive presentation seeks a change in beliefs, attitudes, or behaviour. An entertaining presentation seeks to divert, amuse, or, in some other way, cause listeners to enjoy themselves.
- *Specific Responses:* In addition to the three broad purposes or aims, there are more specific purposes, sometimes referred to as goals or objectives, of speaking. An effective oral presentation has immediate and specific objectives stated in terms of what is expected from the listeners. These specific objectives fall within the broader purposes of information, persuasion, or entertainment. The objectives do not state what the speaker is to do. Rather they tell what the speaker wishes the audience to understand, believe, feel, do, or enjoy.

Gathering Material

With the general purpose and specific objective in mind, you are ready to gather material on the subject. The source for this material should be your own experience or the experience of others gained through conversation, interviews, and written or observed material. You may often draw from all these sources in a single presentation.

- *Self:* The first step in researching an oral presentation is the assembly of all the personal knowledge you have about the subject. A self-inventory may suggest a tentative organization; but, even more important, it will point up gaps in knowledge where you need to do further research.
- *Others:* The second step in the research process is to

draw on the experience of others. People who are interested in the subject provide many ideas during the course of conversation. The most fruitful source, of course, is the expert. Experts help you clarify your thinking, provide facts, and suggest good sources for further research. Their suggestions for further sources can enable you to narrow your search without having to investigate a large bulk of material.

- ***Library:*** The third step is library research. Modern libraries provide us with an abundance of sources—books, newspapers, popular magazines, scholarly journals, abstracts, subject files, microfilms. You must constantly be concerned with the accuracy and relevance of the material. Using material printed in 1950 to understand television today would probably lead to inaccurate, irrelevant conclusions.

Evaluating Material

The next step in the research process is to evaluate the material gathered. You will probably find that you have enough material for several presentations. If you haven't already begun to organize the presentation, you will want to do so. Next you will want to select the best kinds of support for the points you wish to make. Then you will want to prepare a good beginning and ending for the talk.

Organizing The Talk

Clear organization is vital to effective speaking. The most prevalent weakness among speakers at all levels is the failure to organize material for the audience. Speakers have the responsibility to lead listeners mentally from where they are at the beginning of a talk to where they are supposed to be at the end. The message must be organized with the audience in mind; the organization should conform to the thinking processes and expectations of the listeners.

Each speech, lecture, and briefing needs an introduction, a body, and a conclusion. In most instances the introduction and conclusion should be prepared after the body of the talk, since the material in the body is a guide for preparing the introduction and conclusion.

The first consideration in planning the body is how to organize the main points, but organization of subpoints is also important. Arrangement of the main points and subpoints will help both the speaker and the audience remember the material—the speaker while speaking, and the audience while listening.

Most oral presentations, regardless of their length, can be divided into two to five main points. Five is about the maximum number of points from one talk that listeners can be expected to remember.

The most typical ways of organizing main points or subpoints of a talk are by the patterns: time, space, cause/effect, problem/solution, pro/con, or topic. Furthermore, certain strategies can be used with each pattern. How does a speaker decide which patterns and strategies to use? The material will often organize more easily with one pattern and strategy than with another. Consider how various patterns and strategies individually and in combination can be used to organize the main points.

- *Time:* Our vocabularies are filled with words that refer to time: now, tomorrow, yesterday, today, sooner, later, earlier, next (last) week (month, year, time). We work, play, sleep, and eat at certain times. Major events in our lives are organized by time: births, engagements, marriages, deaths. The time, or chronological pattern of organization, then, is a natural way of arranging events in the sequence or order in which they happened or in giving directions on the order to be followed in carrying out those events. This kind of organization is sometimes called *sequential organization.* Certain processes, procedures, or historical movements and developments can often be explained best with a time-sequence organizational pattern.

  The medical technician discussing the mouth-to-mouth system of artificial respiration would probably use a time order for the main points:

- Preliminary steps in preparing the body—proper position, mouth open, tongue and jaw forward,
- The mouth-to-mouth process,
- Caring for the patient once breathing resumes.

Time order is also a logical approach for talks dealing with such subjects as "How to Pack a Parachute," or "How to Prepare a Speech". Furthermore, any talk on a subject with several phases lends itself well to the time pattern. For example, a talk with an objective for the audience to know that the common market was originally planned to develop in three phases might have as main points:

- Phase one, a customs union where nations agreed to reduce duties,
- Phase two, an economic union allowing labourers and goods to move freely across national borders, and
- Phase three, a political union with national representatives as members of a common parliament and using a common currency.

  Of course, rather than looking forward in time from a given moment, the strategy might be to look backward from a point in time. In other words, the strategy might be to move from recent to earlier time rather than from early to late. Regardless of which strategy is used, the flow of the talk and the transitions from one point to the next should make the chronological relationship between main points clear to audience members.

- *Space:* A spatial or geographical pattern is very effective in describing relationships. When using this pattern, the talk is developed according to some directional strategy such as east to west or north to south. For instance, if the speaker were describing the domino theory of Communist infiltration, the strategy would probably be to arrange the main points according to the geographical locations of various nations and how they would be affected by Communist infiltration within their geographical region.

With talks on certain objects, the strategy might be to arrange the main points from top to bottom or bottom to top. A fire extinguisher might be described from top to bottom, an organizational chart from the highest ranking individuals to the lowest ones in the organization, a library according to the services found on the first floor, then the second, and finally those on the third.

Sometimes, the strategy is to organize the talk from the centre to the outside. For example, the control panel in an airplane might be discussed by describing first those often used instruments in the centre, then by moving out toward the surrounding instruments which are used least often.

In all talks arranged spatially, each aspect or main point needs to be introduced according to the strategy used. Just as with a talk organized by time, the subject matter and the transitions should include elaboration and clarification of how the main points relate to one another. A simple listing of the various objects or places without elaboration as to how they are related may confuse the listeners.

- *Cause/Effect:* A causal pattern of arrangement is used in a talk where one set of conditions is given as a cause for another set. In such talks, one of two basic strategies may be used to arrange main points. With a cause/effect strategy you begin with a given set of conditions and contend that these will produce or have already produced certain results or effects; with an effect/cause strategy you take a certain set of conditions as the effects and allege that they resulted from certain causes.

  The cause/effect strategy might be used in a talk concerning the increasing number of women in the Air Force. The talk might first discuss the fact that women are now assuming more responsible leadership roles in the Air Force. One effect of women assuming such roles might be that women are joining the Air Force in increasing numbers.

The effect/cause strategy might be used in a talk on child abuse. The first point might explain the effects of child abuse upon the children themselves, the parents, and even on society. The second point might allege that the causes are that parents themselves were abused as children or that proper education on parenting was not received.

Whichever strategy is used, two cautions must be observed.

- Beware of false causes. Just because one event or circumstance precedes another does not mean that the former causes the latter. Many persons assume that "first A happened, then B took place, so A must have caused B."
- Beware of single causes. Few things result from a single cause. Many causes are more common with one playing on another until it is hard to disentangle them. Lack of safety features on automobiles is not the only cause of most highway accidents; but this cause, plus careless driving or unsafe highways, may account for many highway accidents.

- ***Problem/Solution:*** This pattern, sometimes called the disease/remedy pattern or the need/satisfaction pattern, presents listeners with a problem and then proposes a way to solve it. With this pattern, you must show that a problem exists and then offer a corrective action that is:
  - Practical,
  - Desirable,
  - Capable of being put into action, and
  - Able to relieve the problem.

It must also be one that does not introduce new and worse evils of its own. For example, the issue of controlling nuclear weapons has long been debated.

Those against control argue that erosion of national sovereignty from arms control is more dangerous than no control.

The problem/solution pattern is especially useful with briefings whose purpose is to provide listeners with information on which to base decisions. It can also be used effectively with persuasive speeches and teaching lectures where the speaker wants to present a need or a problem followed by a way or ways to satisfy the need or solve the problem.

There are different strategies that might be employed when using the problem/solution method. If the listeners are aware of the problem and the possible solutions, you will probably discuss the problem briefly, mention the possible solutions, then spend more time in showing why one solution is better than others. For instance, if the objective is for listeners to comprehend that solar energy is the best solution to the energy crisis, our main points might be:

- The world is caught in the grip of an energy crisis.
- Several solutions are possible.
- Solar energy is the best long-term solution.

If the listeners are not aware or are only slightly aware of the problem or need, you may describe in detail the exact nature of the problem. Sometimes, when listeners become aware of the problem, the solution becomes evident and little time is needed to develop the solution. At other times, you may need to spend time developing both the problem and the solution.

Still another strategy is to alternate or stagger portions of the problem with portions of the solution. For example, the cost of a project may be seen as one problem, work-ability another, time to do the projects as a third. Taking up each portion and, in turn, providing solutions to cost, workability, and time as you present these aspects of the problem may be more satisfying to your listeners than if you had discussed all of the problem and then its total solution. The problem/solution pattern is a good one for advocacy or persuasive briefings.

- ***Pro/Con:*** The pro/con pattern, sometimes called the for/against pattern or advantages/dis-advantages pattern, is similar to a problem/ solution pattern in that the talk is usually planned so as to lead to a conclusion. A major difference, however, is that fairly even attention is usually directed toward both sides of an issue with a pro/con pattern.

  There are various strategies to consider when using the pro/con pattern. One consideration is whether to present pro or con first. Another is whether to present both sides and let listeners draw their own conclusions or to present the material in such a way that listeners are led to accept the "school solution". For instance, with a talk on the effects of jogging, you must decide whether to present the advantages or disadvantages first. Then you must decide whether to let listeners make their own decision as to the advantages or disadvantages.

  When deciding the specific strategy to use with the pro/con pattern and determining how much time to spend on each, the following guidelines may be helpful:

  – Giving both sides fairly even emphasis is most effective when the weight of evidence is clearly on the favoured side.
  – Presenting both sides is most effective when listeners may be initially opposed to the school solution.
  – Presenting only the favoured side is most effective when listeners already favour the school solution or conclusion.
  – Presenting the favoured side last makes its acceptance more likely, especially if the other side is not shown in too favourable a light.

- ***Topical:*** A topical division of the main points of a talk involves determining categories of the subject. This type of categorizing or classifying often springs directly from the subject itself. For instance, a talk about a typical college population might be divided into topical divisions of freshmen, sophomores, juniors, and seniors, with each class division serving as a main point. Housing might be discussed in terms of on-base and off-base housing. A talk on the MX intercontinental ballistic missile might be arranged according to the main points of warhead, guidance, and propulsion systems.

At times the material itself suggests certain strategies for ordering the main points. For instance, a talk on lesson planning would most likely begin with knowledge-level planning as the first main point since knowledge-level lessons are generally simpler to understand. Then the lesson would move on through the hierarchy to comprehension, application, analysis, synthesis, and, finally, evaluation levels. In other words your talk would follow a simple-to-complex strategy in organizing the "topics" or levels of lessons.

Other talks might follow strategies of known to unknown, general to specific, or specific to general arrangement of topical main points. There are many strategies for arranging topical main points. The important consideration, as with any pattern, is to give thought to the strategy of arrangement in order to help the listeners' understanding.

- ***Combining Patterns:*** If a single pattern is used to organize the main points, your talks will make more sense. And as a speaker, you will be able to remember more readily what your main points are when you present the talk. Even more important, listeners will be able to follow the talk more easily and remember what you said if a single logical pattern of organization is used for the main points.

  Although you may choose a certain organizational pattern for the main points, you may decide to use different patterns for subpoints. Consider the following tentative outline of a talk with an objective or goal for listeners to know the importance of Non–verbal factors of communication. Notice that the main points (*a*) Performance Factors, and (*b*) Non-performance Factors— are arranged topically. The subpoints for main point (*a*) (upper, middle, and lower body) are organized spatially. A pro/con pattern is followed in discussing positive and negative effects from each body performance factor. The subpoints of main point (*b*) (objects, space, and time) are organized topically. Subpoints under objects are organized by time. Subpoints under space are organized topically.

The important thing to remember is that *each set of main points or subpoints should follow a logical pattern of organization. The tentative outline reflects this fact.* Of course, it may be that none of the formal patterns of organization discussed so far adequately fits your content. For instance, with a speech to entertain, you might simply string together a group of interesting or humorous incidents that would hold the audience's attention. But whatever the case, you must strive to organize your talk in a way that will help you present the information to your listeners in the most meaningful fashion. As you construct a tentative outline, you must do so with your listeners' needs in mind. Quite often, the experienced speaker revises the outline three or four times before being satisfied and finally putting it into final form for the talk.

Now That You Have Organized

The organization patterns and strategies you choose provide structure to the body of your talk. But structure without content is not enough. Interesting and effective supporting material is needed. To use an anatomical analogy, the organization provides the skeleton and the supporting material supplies the flesh for the body of the talk..

Most listeners find it difficult to understand unsupported ideas or assertions. Suppose, for instance, you decide to speak on "How to Organize a Talk". You tell your listeners that they can organize a talk according to one of several possible patterns of presentation. You then tell them that the most common patterns are: time, space, cause/effect, problem/solution, pro/con, and topic. Most likely you will not have provided enough information for your listeners to actually use these patterns of organization.

Factors To Consider For Supporting The Talk

Consider all factors when choosing support. The subject of your talk, the type of talk (briefing, teaching lecture, or speech), and the composition of your audience will help you determine the amount and kinds of support to use.

- *Briefing:* For a briefing, support is generally limited to factual data carefully selected to accomplish the "need to know". The requirement for brevity dictates that you not use extraneous or "nice to know" support. Visual aids are often used to save time and achieve accuracy. Humour is seldom used.

  If the purpose of the briefing is persuasive, use logic rather than emotion to persuade.

- *Teaching Lecture:* Factual material is also important in the teaching lecture, although there may be a need to use support that also appeals strongly to the emotions. Humour and other attention-commanding materials are common throughout the lecture. Visual aids are often used, not only to save time and improve accuracy but also to clarify ideas.

- *Speech:* Informative speeches use much the same support as teaching lectures. Entertaining speeches rely heavily on humour and other attention-getting support. Persuasive speeches are characterized by more appeal to emotions or motives than any other kind of talk you will give. Appeal to such motives as fear, curiosity, loyalty, adventure, pride and sympathy is common in persuasion.

  The distinction between logical and emotional support, however, is in content rather than form. Any type of verbal and visual support may be primarily logical or emotional. But just because support appeals to the emotions does not mean it has to be illogical.

Logical Thinking

Both verbal and visual support, whether used primarily for emotional or logical appeals, should be backed by logical thinking. Here are some problems that commonly affect logical thinking of persons preparing talks.

- ***Slanted Reasoning:*** Slanted reasoning occurs when a speaker makes invalid inferences or reaches false conclusions due to faulty reasoning. Several common types of slanted reasoning follow:
  - The hasty generalization happens when a speaker judges a whole class of objects from an insufficient sample. The person who meets two persons from Mumbai and dislikes them, and based on a sample of two, concludes that all people from Mumbai are unlikable is guilty of making a hasty generalization.
  - The faulty dilemma stems from the fact that although some objects or qualities can be divided into discrete categories, most cannot. Deeds that are not evil are not necessarily good. A cup of coffee may be neither hot nor cold; it may be lukewarm.
  - The faulty analogy happens when a speaker assumes that two things alike in some way or ways are alike in all ways. The human body and an automobile engine are alike in many respects: both must operate within certain temperature limits, both last longer if cared for, both consume fuel. But you would not argue that since adding tetraethyl lead to gasoline makes an automobile engine run better, people should put tetraethyl lead in their coffee.
  - Stacking the evidence occurs when speakers lift out of context only the support that fits their talk while ignoring equally important material that is detrimental to points they are trying to make.

   - Faulty causal reasoning is seen when a speaker reasons that if A is present, B occurs; further if A is absent, B does not occur; therefore, the speaker reasons that A causes B. Of course it could be that B causes A, or perhaps both are caused by a third ingredient, C.

- ***Irrational Appeals:*** Irrational appeals depend upon blind transfer of feelings from one thing to another without logical thought. Consider the following examples of irrational appeal.
   - Name calling refers to putting people or things in a bad light by calling them uncomplimentary names such as fatso, warmonger, nerd, specky etc.
   - Glittering generalities are apparent when speakers wrap their ideas in good, golden, glittering words such as *peace, culture, equality,* and *flag.*
   - Bandwagon appeal operates on the principle that "everyone else is doing it so you should too". Some speakers use the bandwagon appeal to promote the feeling that listeners would be presumptuous to judge for themselves something that the group accepts.
   - "Plain folks" strategy is used when speakers attempt to identify with the simple (and presumably desired) things of life. A speaker who says in front of a farm audience, "I know how you feel, I was born and raised on a farm, and I want to keep the big city politicians' hands off your property tax money," is using plain-folks strategy. Identifying with your audience is a sound practice, but identification alone is not rational support.
   - Prestige or transfer is used by those who drop names or use other strategies to appear important. They believe that simply associating themselves with certain personalities will cause listeners to associate desired traits of those personalities with them as the speakers.

Verbal Support

Verbal support is used either to clarify the points you wish to make or to prove your assertions. Definitions, examples and comparisons are used primarily for clarification. Testimony of experts and statistics can be used either for clarification or proof. Humour can be used with any of the preceding five types of verbal support.

- ***Definitions:*** Definitions are often needed to clarify or explain the meaning of a term, concept, or principle. But like so many words, definition can mean different things and can function in different ways.

  In some talks you may need to use words that are technical, complex, or strange to your listeners. With increasing specialization in both theoretical and applied subjects, the development of new words or terms races ahead of dictionaries. Words such as taxonomy (scientific classification), or groupthink (a problem of groups) might require literal definitions or restatement in simpler language.

  At other times there is a need to define words that are frequently loosely employed. Some words simply have different meanings for different people. Words such as democracy, equal rights, security needs and loyalty can usually be defined easily. For instance, disseminate can be defined very simply as "spread widely". Sometimes a speaker may seek novel and memorable ways to define such terms. Pragmatism might be defined as "a fancy word to mean that the proof of the pudding is in the eating". Sometimes it takes a little longer to fully define what is meant by a certain term.

  Definitions should also be used to explain the meaning of acronyms or abbreviations—words or other combinations of letters formed from the initial letter of each of the successive parts of a compound term.

Finally, at times an entire talk may be needed to define or otherwise introduce students to a new concept or principle—for instance, a speaker discussing the concept of communication as transaction. Perhaps an entire lecture would be needed to explain that the transactional approach means to consider the total communication process and the interaction of the various parts of the process on each other. Other forms of support material such as examples and comparisons would be needed to fully define what was meant.

- ***Examples:*** Any time other persons ask you to "give a for instance", they are asking for an example to clarify the point you are trying to make. Sometimes the examples may be reasonably long. At other times a short example is sufficient. In some cases short examples are similar to definitions. The fact that some support materials might be classed either as definitions or examples should not be a major concern to you. As a speaker, you are more interested in *using* effective support material than in classifying it.

  Often short examples can be clustered together in order to help listeners gain a more complete understanding of the point. In a talk on barriers to effective communication, a speaker might cluster examples of spoonerisms: "Is the bean dizzy?" ("Is the dean busy?"); "I'll have a coff of cuppee" ("I'll have a cup of coffee").

  You should ask yourself several questions about examples you plan to use:

  – Do they accurately represent the point?
  – Will listeners clearly understand their meaning?
  – Do they fit the content? (Avoid those that may confuse.)
  – Will humorous ones add or detract from the lesson?
  – Do they come from personal experience or can other examples be personalized in such a way as to seem real?
  – Can anything be gained from clustering more than three or four examples? Usually not.
  – Do long ones take too much time? (At times,

attention-getting value of long examples may justify their use.)

- Are they interesting?

  The appropriate answers to these questions should be obvious.

- ***Comparisons:*** Description often becomes more graphic when we place an unknown or little understood item beside a similar but better known item. You might want to compare things that are unlike or things that are very much alike.

  Metaphors such as Winston Churchill's "iron curtain" or similes (using the words "like" or "as" such as Robert Burns's "My love is like a red, red rose" or saying "strong as an ox") are comparisons of things that are unlike in most ways. Speakers may compare unlike things. For instance, one might say, "The flow of knowledge is like the relentless and uncompromising flow of a river after the spring thaw as it imposes on us the requirement that we not only adjust to, but anticipate, the future."

  Although analogies that compare dissimilar things serve as an excellent means of clarification, they have limited utility as proof. If you wish to support an assertion, you must compare similar things.

  Contrast is a special form of comparison. For instance, showing how today's standard of living differs from that of a generation ago clarifies and explains a point by showing contrast or differences.

  Obviously, comparisons may be very brief such as those given here or they may be quite long. You need to decide what will work best in a given situation. But whether long or short, comparisons are a valuable and generally underused method of verbal support.

- ***Testimony:*** Words and thoughts of others are particularly useful when you wish to add strong proof support for assertions or points that you make. No one is expected to be an expert on all subjects; speakers often must rely on what others have said. At times testimony of others is used simply to clarify or explain an idea; often it is intended to provide proof for a claim.

If you are presenting a talk on managerial effectiveness in an organization, one of your main points might be the importance of effective downward communication. In other words, you want to stress how important it is for supervisors to keep their subordinates informed. Sometimes, you will want to use direct quotations. At other times you will paraphrase what another has said. Whatever the case, there are two tests of testimony:

- Are the sources competent—do they know what they are talking about? and
- Can they be trusted—are they free from bias? Other considerations are: Is the testimony relevant, clear, and interesting? Are the quotations longer than necessary?

- ***Statistics:*** Statistics are probably the most misused and misunderstood type of verbal support. When properly collected and wisely used, statistics can help speakers clarify their ideas. Statistics are also the most powerful proof support we can use. However, not all figures are statistics, some are simply numbers. Statistics show relationships, largeness or smallness, increases or decreases, or summarize large collections of facts or data. When you choose statistics, there are some questions to ask.

  - Are the statistics recent? Figures concerning the cost of living in 1960 would have limited usefulness for today's family planning its budget. When selecting statistics to use, be on guard if no date is given or if the statistics are outdated.
  - Do the statistics indicate what they purport to? A single test score may not be a true measure of a student's ability. The number of Jets may not indicate the strength of any country's Air Force.

- Do the statistics cover a long enough time or enough samples to be reliable? The results of how one class responded to a new curriculum change would be less meaningful than how three or four classes responded to the change.

  If the statistics are drawn from a sample, does the sample accurately represent the group to which we are generalizing? Public opinion surveys and experimental researchers are generally sensitive to the importance of obtaining a representative sample. Speakers also need to be sensitive to this need.

- When statistics report differences, are the differences significant? Minor variations can often be attributed to chance. In other words, if you were to collect your statistics again, the results might differ.

- When comparing things, are the units of measure compared the same? Failure in one course might have a different meaning than failure in another. If more students fail one course than another, you cannot necessarily conclude that the content of one course is more difficult. Perhaps the grading scale rather than the content was more difficult.

- Do the statistics come from a good, reliable source? And is the source clearly indicated? It is more effective to state the source of the information than to say "recent surveys show".

- Are the statistics presented to their best advantage to aid listener understanding? Could visual aids be used to present the statistics in graphic or tabular form for easier understanding? Have figures been rounded off where possible? Listeners are more likely to remember "nearly 45,000" than "44,871.24". Are the number of statistics limited so that listeners are not overwhelmed by them? Could the significance of statistics be made more clear with meaningful comparisons? To say that World War II cost the United States $200 billion would not be as clearly perceived as if the figures were converted to today's dollars or if they were compared to the cost of a war today using a standard measure.

- ***Humour:*** Most listeners admire a speaker who can use humour effectively. Yet few speakers are able to do so. Moreover, when humour is used, it is generally only at the beginning to gain audience attention. Humour can be used with good results in the body of a talk.

  There are two reasons to use humour in the body of a talk. One is to recapture the attention of the audience. The attention span of most people is only a few minutes; so unless the material is terribly engaging, a speaker can recall instances when an audience's attention wandered. Humour regains attention. The second reason to use humour in the body of a talk is to emphasize an important point. Although a story or anecdote is seldom real proof, it may reinforce your audience's ability to remember the point.

  Humour must be used properly if it is to be effective. There are six essentials to using humour.

  - *Know the item thoroughly:* We have all heard speakers stumble through a potentially humorous item or make it through in fine shape only to forget the punch line. But if speakers know the story and have told it before, they will be able to tell it again and know the kind of response to expect. It is generally a good rule for speakers not to use a story or humorous item of any kind in a speech unless they have told it several times in informal situations so they can both practice and gauge the reactions of others.
  - *Don't use inappropriate humour:* Some speakers consider off-colour stories or ethnic humour as a cheap way to get a laugh from an audience. But

even people who laugh at such stories in private often lose respect for the speaker who uses them in public. Deciding if a joke is inappropriate is not always easy. If there is doubt, the story probably isn't appropriate.

– *Vitalize humour:* Stories should be personalized so they are believable, so they sound as if they really happened. Rather than talk about "this guy I heard about", or "this truck driver," the speaker should give the characters in the stories names. Successful raconteurs and speakers nearly always vitalize their humour.
– *Don't laugh before the audience laughs:* Some comedians get away with laughing first, but good speakers never laugh before the audience. If a speaker fails to get the story across, laughing alone on a platform is disaster. If the joke fails, the speaker is best advised to leave it and go on.
– *Capitalize on the unexpected:* One of the primary elements of humour is that people laugh when they are surprised. The following are all types of humour that depend on the unexpected: quips (of course, men aren't what they used to be—they used to be boys), puns (try our bread, we knead the dough), exaggeration (the heat was so terrific last week that I saw a hound dog chasing a rabbit; they were both walking), understatement (if at first you don't succeed, well, so much for skydiving).
– *See humour in the situation:* The best opportunity for adding humour may come in those minutes just before you speak. It may come from things said by those preceding you on the programme. It may come from malfunction of your visual aids, getting tangled up in the microphone cord, or from a person sneezing in your audience. And although much of this situational humour may not directly support the point you are making, it can nevertheless help win your audience.

Being witty and humorous is not easy. It helps to have an agile and sophisticated mind—one that adapts skillfully to the audience. Yet many more speakers could use humour effectively if they were willing to try and willing to practice.

Visual Support

Verbal support is certainly at the heart of any good talk, but visual aids can function to dramatize, amplify, or clarify the points you are trying to get across to your audience. In this book the emphasis is solely on how to *use* visual aids.

- ***Suggestions:*** Some basic suggestions apply to visual aids that might be used with any type of talk you give.
  - *Use only materials that are relevant*. Avoid using materials solely for aesthetic or interest value. Certainly, visual materials should be interesting, but the primary purpose of any visual aid is to portray or support an idea graphically for your listeners. Irrelevant materials distract from the idea you are presenting.
  - *Use visual materials that are large enough to be seen by all the audience*. Nothing is so disturbing as to be seated in the back of the room unable to see the visual aids. In preparing for your talk, display the visual aids, then move yourself to the location of your most distant listener. If you can't readily see the material, consider replacing it with something more appropriate.
  - *Use visual materials only at the proper time*. Do not expose the visual material until the proper point in the talk. Clearly mark your notes or outline so you will know when to use each piece of visual support. Materials that are visible too soon or that remain in view after the point has been made distract from and interrupt the continuity of the talk. You may want to use the "striptease" or buildup method for revealing a series of points. Don't list ten main points for the audience and then

discuss each one. Instead, uncover the points one at a time to keep the audience's attention focused.

- *Keep visual materials as simple and as clear as possible.* Emphasize only the most important information. Omit unnecessary details. A series of simple charts is preferable to a single complicated one.
- *Talk to the audience, not to the visual aid.* If you are explaining a chart, look at your audience as much as possible. By the time you make your talk, you should be so familiar with your visual aids that it will be unnecessary for you to look at them closely. When possible, paraphrase the visual material instead of reading it, or pause and let the audience read it silently.
- *Place visual aids away from obstructions.* Don't allow other projects or persons—including yourself—to obstruct the view of your audience. You decided to use visual materials to support and clarify your talk. Don't hinder their effectiveness by obstructing the audience's view.
- *If you plan to use equipment* such as an overhead projector, a slide projector, or a film projector, *make certain beforehand that you know how to use the equipment and that it is set up and ready to go.* Also, know whether or not you have a spare bulb, how to change it, or how to improvise and do without the equipment. In other words, be ready for any contingencies that may develop. Many potentially sound presentations fail because the speaker fails to plan for equipment that malfunctions.
- *When using flipcharts, consider flipping from back to front rather than from front to back.* There are at least three advantages. First, flipping back to front is easier—try it if you don't think so. Second, flipping from back to front can be done from the side of the charts rather than from the front—between the

charts and the audience—as you generally have to do when flipping from front to back. Third, if the paper you use for the charts is relatively thin, the back to front procedure prevents your audience from reading through the paper to a chart you haven't yet discussed.

- Finally, before you construct a visual aid, ask yourself if the effort and expense required to prepare or procure the aid are justified and add significantly to the overall value of the talk. If not, forget it. Often the time spent preparing visual aids could be better spent preparing and practicing the talk.

- ***Using a Chalkboard:*** If you use a chalkboard, consider the following additional suggestions:
  - Pare the chalk to desired thickness so that the lines you draw are 1/4 to 3/8 inches wide. Have spare pieces of chalk ready for use.
  - Use a No. 2 soft pencil and yardstick to make erasable guidelines on the board before your audience enters the room. Later when writing on the board during your talk you can ensure straight and even lettering by following lines invisible to your audience.
  - Cramping your letters and diagrams cramps your speaking. To be seen easily at 30 feet, letters should be about three inches high.
  - Avoid using the bottom half of the board if you are speaking from the same floor level as your audience since some listeners may be unable to see.
  - Determine where glare on the board is a distraction. Before the audience enters the room adjust window shades or avoid these areas of the board.
  - If the room is equipped with a magnetic chalkboard, or if some other metal surface such as a file cabinet is nearby, consider preconstructed

visual aids with magnets glued to the back. Reusable magnetic material one-inch wide can be purchased in long lengths and cut easily to the desired length. Two magnets one-inch square will support one square foot of lightweight illustration board.

After You Have Your Support

By this time you have considered the unique factors of your talk. You have decided whether to present a briefing, a lecture, or some type of speech. You have considered your audience, your subject, your objectives and have gathered your material. You have organized the body of the talk and have selected the kinds of verbal and visual support you will use with careful thought toward being logical in your use of support. Two important ingredients must be supplied before you are ready to work on presenting your talk. You need to plan a good introduction and a good conclusion.

Beginning And Ending The Talk

Once you have organized and supported the body of the talk with appropriate verbal and visual materials, you must decide how to begin and end. For many persons, beginning (or providing an introduction to the body of the talk) and ending (providing a conclusion) is most troublesome. Introductions and conclusions should fit the audience, the speaker, and the type of talk you are giving.

Briefing

Since briefings are to be brief, lengthy introductions and conclusions are inappropriate.

- *Introduction:* Your listeners need and want to know about your subject; therefore, you will not need to spend time getting their attention. If, as often happens, another speaker introduces you and your subject, you need only give a quick overview of the subject and proceed immediately to the main points. Your listeners' familiarity with the subject will determine the length of the overview. In most cases simply mentioning the main points is sufficient. If you are not introduced, you might simply say, "Good morning, I'm ______________ briefing on ______________."

- *Conclusion:* This part of a briefing should be short but positive. If your briefing is to stop with a listing of possible solutions or courses of action, a brief listing or summary of your points can give a sense of completion. If your briefing ends with a conclusion, as in a staff study report, you may end with a brief, clear restatement of the possible solution you judge best. No new material or commentary should be presented here. Or you may conclude by making a short statement recommending the action that would put your solution into effect.

Although many briefings are subject to interruption for questions from listeners, many times a good concluding sentence might be: "Ladies and Gentlemen, are there any (further) questions?" If a question period is not to follow, or once the questions have ended, you might simply say, "Ladies and Gentlemen, that concludes my briefing." At other times, the ranking person listening to the briefing may conclude the question period for you by declaring, "We have no further questions."

Teaching Lecture

Introductions and conclusions to teaching lectures are very important. Much care should be given to their development and use.

- *Introduction:* The introduction to a teaching lecture should serve several purposes: to establish a common ground between the instructor and students, to capture and hold attention, to outline the lecture and relate it to the overall course, to point out benefits to the students, and to lead the students into the lecture content. Although humour may be appropriate, the introduction should be free of irrelevant stories, jokes, or incidents that distract from the lesson objective, and it should not contain long or apologetic remarks that are likely to dampen student interest in the lesson. Educators often speak of three necessary elements in the introduction of a lecture: gain attention, motivate, and provide an overview of material to be covered in the lecture.

- *Attention:* To gain attention, the instructor may tell a story that relates to the subject and provides a background for the lecture. Another approach may be to make an unexpected or surprising statement or ask a question that relates the lecture to group needs. A rhetorical question (Have you ever... ? or, Can you imagine... ?) might be effective. At other times, nothing more than a clear indication that the lecture has begun is sufficient. In all instances, the primary concern is to focus student attention on the subject. .
- *Motivation:* You should use the introduction to discuss specific reasons why the students need to learn whatever you want them to learn. In this motivational discussion, you should make a personal appeal to students and reinforce their desire to learn. The appeal may relate the learning to career advancement, financial gain, service to the community, use at home, or to some other need, but in every instance, you should cite a specific application for student learning experiences. In many cases, the need for this lecture as a foundation for future lessons is strong motivation. This motivational appeal should continue throughout the lecture. If you briefly mention student needs only in the introduction, you are square-filling, not motivating.
- *Overview:* For most instructional methods, the introduction should provide an overview of what is to be covered during the class period. A clear, concise presentation of the objective and key ideas serves as a road map for the learning route. Effective visual aids can be helpful at this point.

A clear overview can contribute greatly to a lecture by removing doubts in the minds of the learners about where the lesson is going and how they are going to get there. Students can be told what will be covered or left out and why. They can be informed about how the ideas have been organized. Research shows that students understand better and retain more when they know what to expect. The purpose of the overview is to prepare students to listen to the body of the lecture.

- ***Conclusion:*** The conclusion of a lecture may stick with the students longer than anything else said. For this reason you should give much care to its preparation. The conclusion of most lectures should accomplish three things: summarize, remotivate, and provide closure.
   - *Final summary:* Mini or interim summaries may be appropriate at various places in a lecture—for instance, after each main point has been made. But final summaries come after all main points of the lecture have been made. An effective final summary retraces the important elements discussed in the body. As the term suggests, a final summary reviews the main points of the lecture in a concise manner. By reviewing the main points, it can aid students' retention of information and give them a chance to fill in missing information in their notes.
   - *Remotivation:* The purpose of the remotivation is to instill in students a desire to retain and use what they have learned. Effective instructors provide motivation throughout the lecture. But the remotivation step is the instructor's last chance to let students know why the information presented in the lecture is so important to the student as an individual. Perhaps it is important because it provides the groundwork for future lessons or because it will help them do their jobs more

effectively. But whatever the reasons given, they should be ones that appeal directly to the students and show the importance to them of what was learned.

– *Closure:* For many instructors the closure presents a difficult challenge. The students need to be released from listening. Sometimes instructors at a loss on how to close say, "Well that's about all I have to say," or "I guess I don't have anything else." This type of closure is not very satisfying. There are much more effective ways of closing. Sometimes vocal inflection can signal that the lecture is ending. Quotations, stories, or humorous incidents can also provide effective closure. Sometimes when the lecture is to be followed by other lessons in the same block of instruction, you might say something such as "Next time, then, we will continue with our discussion of Between now and then if you have any questions, come to my office and I'll see if I can answer them for you."

Speech

All speeches need introductions and conclusions. But the types of introductions and conclusions needed may differ greatly from speech to speech.

- ***Introduction:*** For many speeches you will most likely want to use the same three steps of attention, motivation, and overview that you would use for a teaching lecture. There are times, however, when such an introduction might not be appropriate.

  At times an attention step may not be needed. A war hero talking to a local veterans organization, a prominent family counsellor speaking to a group of married couples who chose to attend the talk all have their audiences' attention at the beginning. Still, attention of the audiences is not something that can be taken for granted. Although keeping attention is not always an easy task, it is not as difficult as initially gaining the attention.

If you can't decide whether or not you need an attention step in your speech, then you probably do. Most talks will be improved with the addition of an effective attention step.

Although some sort of attention device is usually needed in a speech, at times a motivation step may be unnecessary. For instance, if your listeners are highly motivated to listen, then a motivation step establishing their need to listen would be out of place or redundant at best.

Every good speaker, of course, attempts to motivate listeners throughout the speech. No matter how much credibility you have on the subject or how willing your audience is to listen to you, you have a responsibility to provide continuing motivation for them to listen throughout the talk.

The overview step needed in most teaching lectures is unnecessary in many speeches. In fact, with speeches to persuade it may be advantageous if you do not preview what is to follow—especially if the audience does not initially share your point of view. If speakers tell their audiences what they want to persuade them to believe or do, they may turn audiences against them before they even begin.

Also, the material in some speeches—such as some speeches to entertain—may not lend itself to an overview. Generally, in an informative speech, some type of overview is helpful, even if the overview consists only of mentioning the main points or telling them what you are going to tell them. The best advice is to consider the audience, occasion, and objectives of your speech, then decide if an overview is appropriate.

- *Conclusion:* In some speeches you may choose to use the same three steps of summary, remotivation, and closure appropriate for teaching lectures. As with the introduction, however, the speaking situation will help determine what kind of conclusion is best.

Most speeches will not require an extensive conclusion. With informative speeches you may want to summarize briefly the main points you covered. With persuasive speeches, your conclusion may be a motivating statement of what you want your listeners to believe or how you want them to act. With an entertaining speech there may be little to actually summarize or motivate about.

All kinds of speeches, however, need some type of closure to provide completeness. Most speakers seem to give little thought to how to conclude. You can be assured that the time you spend attending to this detail will be time well spent since it is the last impression that the audience often carries with them when you have finished.

□□

Chapter 8

Gaining Attention

Although different types of talks require different kinds of introductions, some general suggestions may be helpful. Many of the following suggestions will be useful for gaining attention in lectures and speeches. You will have to decide which ones apply to the talk you are giving.

QUESTION

You will want your audience to respond in one of two ways. If you begin with a question—"What has been the most significant event in your life?"—you will not expect an audible answer, for the question is a rhetorical one. But you do expect your audience to think of an answer. The other type of question is one in which you expect an answer. The purpose is to get a unified audience reaction. "Do you want to keep on paying high taxes?" The politician using this question may want the audience to respond in unison, "No!"

Questions are easy to design. Good questions are a little more difficult. "Have you ever wondered how many people drive Maruti 800?" is not a good question. Many people in your audience reply mentally, "No, and I don't care". A question such as "Would you like to earn a million next week?" is also ineffective since it is pretty far from reality. You should also avoid confusing questions: "How much fuel was used by the Indian Air Force, and all commercial airlines during the past five years?"; and questions that may embarrass: "How many of you are deeply in debt?"

Good questions are clear and direct and invite involvement from the audience: "If you had one wish, what would it be?"

QUOTATION

Usually without looking too hard, you can find someone both authoritative and popular who is enthusiastic and supports your point of view. Or if you speak often, you may wish to invest in one of the many specialized paperback versions on the market. There are quotation books especially for teachers, salesmen, speakers, ministers, and others. Also, if you keep your eyes open, you will come across quotations in your day-to-day reading that you can use later on. Make it a practice to write them down and file them away for future use. When you do use a quotation to open a talk, remember to keep it brief and understandable. You want to gain the audience's attention, not lose it.

JOKE

Many speakers would be well advised not to open with a joke. When you buy a joke book from the local bookstore or check one out from the library, you find nothing but old gags about in-laws, drunks, and talking horses. A comedian or skilled raconteur can make the jokes funny with appropriate lead-in lines, timing, and putting the story into a believable context.

If you do wish to use a joke or humorous story, read again the suggestions for using humour given earlier in this book. Especially attend to the suggestion to tell the story several times before using it in the talk so that you know it well and know the kind of response to expect. Also remember to make sure the story adds rather than detracts from your talk by making certain it is relevant, humorous, and not offensive to your audience. Many speakers have put themselves at serious disadvantage at the beginning of their talk by failing to consider these things.

STARTLING STATEMENT

"Tonight more people will watch a Ramayana on TV than have seen all of the stage performances of all of Shakespeare's plays in the last 400 years". (This happens to be a true statement.) "When I was 13 years old I fell in love with a woman 37 feet tall". This statement would be a novel way to start a talk about a 37-

foot statue in one's hometown. Remember to make your statement not only startling, but relevant.

GIMMICK

Novelty openings are distinctive, creative, and usually visual. Gimmicks such as tearing a five-dollar bill in half, blowing a loud whistle, or taking off one's coat and hurling it across the room may be illegal, dangerous, or simply not relevant. Think through any gimmick that you plan to use. Try it on a few friends first to get their reaction. Then make certain it is legal, safe, and relevant to your talk.

COMMON GROUND

A speaker establishes common ground by mentioning a common interest relevant to the subject at hand. This technique should be distinguished from the "plain-folks" appeal. Unlike the politician who reminds his audience that he too was born and raised on a farm—a claim that may be true but is probably unrelated to his topic—common ground is established on a point relevant to the talk. And it is sincere. When visiting a university at which he once was a student, a professor might begin: " It is a real pleasure to be in Delhi City, to visit again this university where I received two degrees, and to have the opportunity to renew so many happy and precious friendships. It was here that many of my ideas about communication theory and public speaking were formed".

REFERENCE

Many times you can gain the audience's attention simply by referring to the occasion, significance of the subject, special interest of the audience, or what a previous speaker has said.

Occasion

During our country's 60th Republic the Prime Minister began: "We are assembled to celebrate the 60th Republic Day of India". A speech commemorating the world's first night flight in Montgomery, Alabama, began: "Today we are gathered on a very historic spot. It was here at the Wright Flying School that the first successful night flight was completed."

Subject

The method of referring to the subject is closely related to the earlier comments concerning the motivation step appropriate for the lecture. The method is simple. Develop the attention around the implied theme: My subject is important to you now. In other words, tell the listeners why they should listen to you. This approach is most successful when you do not actually tell the listeners why the subject is important, since actually telling them often results in a colourless, trite statement. You simply think of the two or three reasons why the subject is significant, then state and amplify them until the audience reacts favourably. A slight variation is to start something like this: "I am not afraid that you will underestimate the importance of what I have to say today, for the subject of _______________ concerns everybody."

Special Interests

A speaker addressing a local Lions Club known for its support of the Cricket game each year to raise money for the eye bank programme might start: "The cricket game is enjoyed annually through nationwide TV. But how many of its viewers know that it is more than a game with some of this country's finest professional prospects? All of us in this room know that this game helps people see."

Previous Speaker

When several speakers appear on one occasion, an alert speaker can often shape an opening based on what someone else has already said. This means is particularly effective since the reference is fresh in the listeners' minds and gives a sense of spontaneity to the talk. If you use this approach you can either explain how your subject fits with the previous talk or show a plausible relation between the two. For example, you may begin by saying "Mrs Dolly just told, you __________. I am going to speak in a different support idea".

TRANSITIONS AND INTERIM SUMMARIES

Transitions and interim summaries can be used to help the audience understand the continuity of thought and focus on main ideas.

Transitions

Transitions are statements used by the speaker to move from the introduction to the body of the talk, between main points, between subpoints within each main point, and from the body to the conclusion of the talk. Transitions signal to the audience that you are progressing to a new point, but they are also important in maintaining the continuity of the information being given. Consider this transition:

"We have discussed the precedents for a mandatory physical fitness programme in the police force. Next we will consider the benefits of such a programme."

This transition indicates a change in direction, but it does not indicate the reason for or importance of the change.

For transitions to be effective, they should

- Mention the point just discussed,
- Relate that point to the objective of the talk, and
- Introduce the next point.

Now Consider this transition.

We have discussed the precedents for a mandatory physical fitness programme in the police force, but these precedents alone will not prove a need for such a programme. To more fully understand that need, we must next examine in several practical situations the benefits of mandatory physical fitness."

When planned and used correctly, transitions act as "mini-summaries" and contribute substantially to the continuity of the total talk.

Interim Summaries

Summaries after main points or key ideas are useful tools for maintaining continuity within a talk and for highlighting areas of particular impor-tance. Interim summaries are not always necessary in a talk. In fact, if the point is very clear, a summary may be unnecessarily redundant and boring. You should use them, however, when main points are unusually long or contain complex or unfamiliar information. With interim summaries you repeat information concisely and reinforce audience understanding before new information is presented. Interim summaries should not take the place of transitions; they should provide a means for you to progress logically from one main point, through the transition, and into the next point.

□□

Chapter 9

Presentation of the Talk

The most frightening and the hardest part for many people is the actual presentation of the talk although preparing a talk can be laborious. Questions speakers most often ask are: "How many notes should I use?" "How can I overcome nervousness?" "What kind of physical behaviour is appropriate for me to use when I speak?" "What if my voice isn't suited to speaking before a group? "How can I project sincerity and enthusiasm?" Answers to these questions will provide whatever follows below.

PRESENTATION METHODS

Speakers can use one of the four common methods for presentation:

- Speaking from memory,
- Reading from manuscript,
- Speaking impromptu with no specific preparation, and
- Speaking extemporaneously with, ideally, a great deal of preparation and a limited number of notes.

The fourth method usually allows us the most freedom in adjusting to an audience as we speak.

Memorizing

Speaking from memory is the poorest method of delivering talks, and it should be used very sparingly or not at all. While this method may seem to be helpful for persons who cannot think on their feet, the memorized talk is a straitjacket. Such a talk cannot be adapted to the immediate situation or audience reactions. In other words, it does not allow the speaker to adjust to the particular situation. Moreover, the method is almost sure to destroy spontaneity and a sense of communication. The method also requires an inordinate amount of preparation, and the danger of forgetting is ever present.

Manuscript Reading

Reading a talk from a manuscript allows for planning the exact words and phrases to use. But the disadvantages of this method of presentation far outweigh the advantages. Many speakers use the manuscript as a crutch instead of fully thinking through the ideas in the talk. All too often the written talk is regarded simply as an essay to be read aloud. Therefore, the talk is too broad and has language that is too abstract to be understood when presented orally.

If you must read from a manuscript, consider the following suggestions:

- ***Prepare the Manuscript:***
  - Spoken words should be simpler, clearer, and more vivid than writing.
  - Sentences should be shorter and ideas less complex than in writing.
  - Transitions between thoughts and ideas need to be clear. Provide signposts to keep the audience from getting lost.
  - Use repetition to emphasize main ideas and key points.
  - Use direct address when speaking about people. Personal pronouns such as *I, we, our, us, you,* are better than *they, people, a person, the reader, the hearer.*
  - Use concrete language where possible. Follow abstract or complicated reasoning with specific examples, comparisons, and definitions.

- ***Prepare a Reading Draft:***
  - Use as large a type as possible. Special type two or three times larger than ordinary will greatly enhance visibility.
  - Double or triple space to make the words stand out more clearly and reduce chances for confusion or misreading of the text.
  - Type on only one side of the paper to facilitate handling.
  - Mark your manuscript, perhaps using vertical lines between words where you wish to pause. Underscore words you want to emphasize. Some speakers use double and triple vertical lines or underlining for added emphasis.
  - Mark places in the manuscript where you plan to use visual aids.
  - Use short paragraphs to reduce the chance of losing your place.
  - Some speakers vary the length of line according to meaning.
- ***Practice the Talk:***
  - Read the talk aloud to see how it sounds. Recording yourself on a cassette recorder and listening to the playback will help you to discover places where you may not be communicating effectively.
  - Read and reread the talk several times, perhaps once a day for several days if you have time.
  - Try to make your talk sound like conversation, as if you were thinking the words for the first time as you read them.
  - Avoid combinations of words that are difficult to say. Make necessary changes on the manuscript.
  - Practice looking at your audience most of the time as the manuscript becomes more familiar to you.

- Provide the punctuation with vocal inflection, variety, and pauses.

- ***Presenting the Talk:***

Use one of two methods for handling the manuscript. (*a*) Hold the manuscript in front of you with one hand high enough so that you can see it without bending your head, but not high enough to hide your face. The other hand will be free to turn pages and gesture. (*b*) Place the manuscript on a speaker's stand or table so that both hands are free to gesture. Make sure, however, that the manuscript is placed high enough to read from without bending over. Sometimes books or other objects may be used to raise the manuscript to the desired height. Whichever method is used, remember to *let the eyes, not the head, drop to the paper.*

- Don't explain why you choose to read the talk. If you have prepared well, you should do a good job and no apologies will be necessary.
- Be willing to change the wording here and there as you go along if it will help you communicate ideas to your hearers. These changes will make delivery more conversational.
- Insert comments of up to a sentence or two in length to add variety, but be careful not to deviate so far from the manuscript that your train of thought is interrupted. You should have carefully thought through and prepared the manuscript. Last minute changes and impromptu asides can be confusing both for you and your hearers.
- Be flexible enough so that you can shorten the talk if necessary.
- Let pauses be dictated by ideas. Pause wherever there would normally be a pause in the same language in informal conversation. You will need to pause often, even when the written punctuation does not dictate a pause.

- Concentrate on the meaning and ideas rather than on individual words. If you have written your own talk, you are intimate with the ideas and the words you chose to express them. You built the talk, you should understand it. Therefore, the most helpful aid to good delivery is to recreate the feeling that helped you put the words on paper. Speak no passage until its meaning hits your mind.
- Construct the next idea in your mind before uttering it.
- Read with all the sincerity, enthusiasm, directness, and force that is proper to the occasion.
- Use gestures and look directly at the audience when executing them.

A manuscript talk, then, is not, as someone once said, merely "an essay on its hind legs". The manuscript should be written in a conversational tone rather than formal English. It is meant to be heard, not read. If you prepare well, practice diligently, and attend to factors of delivery, you can usually read very acceptably and spontaneously.

Impromptu

You may find it necessary at times to talk on the spur of the moment without any preparation. Speaking impromptu requires a tremendous amount of skill and knowledge. But this method should be used only by experienced speakers who are saturated with their subjects and who have the ability to organize their thoughts for learning as they speak. They have spent years, so to speak, in preparing to give an unprepared talk. Even these experienced speakers fall back upon thoughts and phrases they have used before.

Extempore

The talk is carefully planned and outlined in detail. The technique effective speakers use most widely, extemporaneous speaking, produces the most fruitful results when it is based upon full preparation and adequate practice. It is a lesson planned idea by idea rather than word by word. The speaker's only guide is usually a well-constructed outline.

The advantages of speaking from a well-planned outline are many. It gives freedom to adapt a talk to the occasion and to adjust to audience reactions. It enables speakers to change what they plan to say right up to the moment of utterance. In short, the extemporaneous method will permit the speaker to adhere to the two vital needs of effective speaking: adequate preparation and a lively sense of communication. The method compels speakers to organize ideas and puts pressure on them to weigh materials in advance.

This brief outline may be thought of as a *keyword* outline with keywords and key phrases to remind you of main points, subpoints, support material you plan to use, questions you might ask, and the things you want to mention in the introduction and conclusion. You may want to prepare two versions of the outline. One version will be very complete—almost in manuscript form—so you can return to it several weeks or months later if you are called upon to give a similar talk. Another version will be much briefer—perhaps only one page long, or written on cards so you can use it when you actually give your talk.

- ***Keyword Outline:*** The keyword outline should be divided into three main parts: introduction, body, and conclusion. As discussed previously, the introduction may have three subparts: attention, motivation, and overview. The body will have the main points of the talk as major subdivisions. The conclusion may have three subdivisions: final summary, remotivation, and closure.
- ***Symbol System:*** To show the relative importance of lesson materials in the body of the lesson, you might use a number or letter symbol before each entry. But some rules of outlining to remember are:
  - Only one symbol should be used per point or idea.
  - Subordinate points should be indented.
  - The principle of subpoints or subordination means

that a point follows logically or supports the point above it.

As you can see from the keyword outline, the speaker plans to seek the audience's attention by using a familiar quotation—"actions speak louder than words"—and then use an example about a "dinner jacket". The speaker plans to provide motivation by giving testimony from an expert concerning the amount of the message that is communicated non–verbally. Then the speaker plans to use a visual aid—an overview chart—that outlines the main points of the talk.

The two main points—know the performance factors of non–verbal communication and know the non–performance factors of non–verbal communication—are arranged topically. The subpoints under the first main point (upper body, middle body, and lower body) are arranged spatially—from top to bottom. Each of the sub–subpoints (head-eyes-facial expression; arms-hands-torso; hips-legs-feet) are also arranged spatially—from top to bottom.

The subpoints under second main point (objects, space, and time) are arranged topically. The sub–subpoints under objects are arranged according to time, and sub–subpoints under space seem to be arranged topically.

Notice also that the speaker has written keywords not only for main points, subpoints, and sub–subpoints but also has written enough down to remember the support that will be used. Some speakers also like to write in their suggested transitions. While writing of the transitions may inhibit spontaneity, the practice is often preferable to having weak or no transitions.

Obviously, when preparing your notes for your talk you will want to use what works best for you. This sample outline is only intended as a possible way of preparing your notes.

NON–VERBAL COMMUNICATION

Nervousness

If you suffer from stage fright, nervousness, or fear of speaking, your audience may also become uneasy or anxious. Yet some nervousness is both natural and desirable. Even skilled speakers often experience the queasy feeling of "butterflies in the stomach" as they prepare to speak. The secret is to get the butterflies "flying in formation", through practice. Just as a visiting athletic team practices on a field before game time to accustom themselves to differences in terrain and environment, so you may need to dry run or practice your talk several times, preferably in the room where the talk will be given, before actually presenting it. Practice reminds us to look up the pronunciation of a word that is new or check an additional piece of information on an important point.

Suggestions For Nervous Speakers

Consider the following suggestions for coping with nervousness.

- It is important to be enthusiastic about your subject, because enthusiasm can replace fear. Enthusiasm is the key when practice is over and you are ready to deliver the talk. At times you may talk on subjects that you find dull, but as you get more involved, the subject becomes more interesting. There is no such thing as a dull subject, only dull speakers. And the more enthusiastic you are about the subject, the more involved the audience will be both with you and what you are saying.
- The listeners in the audience are the same ones that you enjoy speaking with in a less structured environment. Most audiences are made up of warm human beings with an interest in what you have to say. Hold good thoughts toward your audience. They rarely boo or throw vegetables. Most listeners have great empathy for speakers and want them to do a good job.

- Do not rush as you begin to speak. Many speakers are so anxious to get started that they begin before they are really ready. The little extra time taken to arrange your notes will generally pay big dividends. When you are ready to begin, look at various parts of the audience, take a deep breath, and begin to speak.

PHYSICAL BEHAVIOUR

Communication experts tell us that over half of our meaning may be communicated non–verbally. Although non–verbal meaning is communicated through vocal cues, much meaning is carried by the physical behaviours of eye contact, bodily movement, and gestures. You need to know how these physical behaviours can improve your speaking skill.

Eye Contact

Eye contact is one of the most important factors of non–verbal communication. Nothing will enhance your delivery more than effective eye contact with your audience. Eye contact is important for three reasons.

- It lets the listeners know that you are interested in them. Most people like others to look at them when talking.
- Effective eye contact allows you to receive non–verbal feedback from your audience. With good eye contact, you can gauge the effect of your remarks. You can determine if you are being understood and which points are making an impact and which are not. You will be able to detect signs of poor understanding and signs that the listeners are losing interest. Then you can adjust your rate of delivery or emphasis. You can rephrase or summarize certain points or add more supporting data.
- Effective eye contact enhances your credibility. Speakers with the greatest eye contact are judged by listeners as being more competent.

You must have an earnest desire to communicate with them. To achieve genuine eye contact, you must do more than merely look in the direction of your listeners. The old advice of looking over the tops of your listeners' heads or attempting to look at all parts of the audience systematically simply does not describe effective eye contact. Furthermore, looking at only one part of the audience or directing attention only to those listeners who seem to give you reinforcing feedback may cause you to ignore large parts of the audience.

Make it evident to each person in a small group and each part of the audience in larger auditoriums that you are interested in them as individuals and eager to have them understand the ideas you are presenting. Effective eye contact can be described as *direct* and *impartial.* You look directly into the eyes of your listeners, and you look impartially at all parts of the audience, not just at a chosen few. In this way you will establish mental as well as sensory contact with your listeners.

Body Movement

Good body movement is important because it catches the eye of the listener. It is one of the important factors of dynamic and meaningful physical behaviour. It helps to hold the attention needed for good communication. But movement can also represent a marked departure or change in your delivery pattern—a convenient way of punctuating and paragraphing your message. Listeners will know that you are finished with one idea or line of thought and ready to transition to the next. Finally, aside from its effects on the listeners, movement helps you as a lecturer. It helps you work off excess energy that can promote nervousness. Movement puts you at ease.

Some speakers never move yet are quite effective. However unless the formality of the situation or the need to use a fixed microphone keeps you in one position, then you probably should move frequently. Movement from behind the lectern can reduce the psychological distance between you and your listeners and place them more at ease.

Some speakers feel that they need the lectern to hold their notes. But in most cases it is actually more effective if you carry your notes with you rather than looking down at the lectern to see them. But whenever you look at your notes, remember to *drop your eyes not your head.* In other words, have your notes high enough that you can see them.

Effective body movement can be described as *free* and *purposeful.* You should be free to move around in front of the listeners. You should not feel restrained to stay behind the lectern but should move with reason and purpose. Use your movement to punctuate, direct attention, and otherwise aid communication.

Of course, some speakers move too much. Perhaps out of nervousness they pace back and forth in front of the audience. Still others have awkward movement that does not aid communication. Some leave their notes on the lectern then move in and out from behind it like a hula dancer. Others plant their feet firmly in one place then rock from one side to the other in regular cadence.

Gestures

By gestures we mean the purposeful use of the hands, arms, shoulders, and head to reinforce what is being said. Gestures may be used to clarify or emphasize ideas. Fidgeting with a paper clip, rearranging and shuffling papers, and scratching your ear are not gestures. They are not purposeful and they distract from the verbal message. Placing both hands in your pockets, or behind your back, or in front of you in a fig leaf position severely limits their use for gesturing. Holding your shoulders and head in one position during the talk will also rob you of an effective means of strengthening your communication.

Although gestures can be perfected through practice, they will be most effective if you make a conscious effort to relax your muscles before you speak, perhaps by taking a few short steps or unobtrusively arranging your notes. Effective gestures are complete and vigourous. Many speakers begin to gesture, but perhaps out of fear, they do not carry through and their gestures abort. Comedians get laughs from the audience by timing gestures improperly. A gesture that comes after the word or phrase is spoken appears ludicrous.

You should not adopt a dynamic, forceful mode of delivery if by nature you are quiet and reserved. As with movement, gestures should spring from within. Effective gestures are both *natural* and *spontaneous.* Observe persons talking with each other in a small group. You should try to approximate the same naturalness and spontaneity of gestures when you are speaking.

Good gestures should come exactly at the time or slightly before the point is made verbally. Poor timing results from attempting to "can" or pre-plan gestures. Finally, good gestures are versatile. A stereotyped gesture will not fit all subjects and situations. Furthermore, the larger the audience, the more pronounced the gestures will need to be. As with all aspects of communication, gestures must fit the situation.

USE OF VOICE

Three major characteristics of a good voice is that it is reasonably pleasant, it is easily understood, and it expresses differences in meaning. Technically we might label these three properties as quality, intelligibility, and variety.

Quality

Certainly a pleasing quality or tone is a basic component of a good speaking voice. Quality refers to the overall impression a voice makes on others. Some persons have a full rich quality, others one that is shrill and nasal, and still others may have a breathy and muffled tone or quality. Although basic aspects of quality may be difficult to change, your voice may become more breathy when you are excited, tense when suspense is involved, and resonant when reading solemn language. Listeners can often tell from the voice if the speaker is happy, angry, sad, fearful, or confident. Similarly vocal quality can convey sincerity and enthusiasm. Some speakers are overly concerned about the basic quality of their voices, but at the same time they pay too little attention to the effect of attitude and emotion on the voice.

Intelligibility

Intelligibility or understandability of your speech depends on several factors.

- A synonym of articulation is enunciation. Articulation refers to the precision and clarity with which sounds of speech are uttered. Good articulation is chiefly the job of the jaw, tongue, and lips. Most articulation problems result from laziness of the tongue and lips or failure to open the mouth wide enough. What sounds like overarticulation to you will come out as crisp, understandable words and phrases to your listeners. You should overarticulate rather than underarticulate your speech sounds.

- Traditional or customary utterance of words is referred to as pronunciation. Standards of pronunciation differ, making it difficult at times to know what is acceptable. Dictionaries are useful, but as they become outdated, they should not be adhered to excessively. Generally, educated people in your community as well as national radio and television announcers provide a good standard for pronunciation. Common faults of pronunciation are to misplace the accent (saying *de*-vice instead of de-*vice*), to omit sounds (guh/mnt for government), to add sounds (ath*a*lete for athlete), and to sound silent letters (mor*t*gage or of*t*en). Remember that pronunciation acceptable in informal conversation may be substandard when speaking in front of a group. Do not overcompensate to the point that you call attention to your speech.

- Vocalized pause is the name we give to syllables "a," "uh," "um," and "ah" often at the beginning of a sentence. While a few vocalized pauses are natural and do not distract, too many impede the communication process.

- Overuse of stock expressions such as "OK", "like", and "you know" should be avoided. These expressions serve no positive communicative function and only convey a lack of originality by the speaker.

- Substandard grammar has no place in speaking. It will only serve to reduce your credibility with some listeners. Research shows that even persons who have been using substandard grammar all of their lives can, with diligent practice, make significant gains in this area in a relatively short time.

Variety

Listeners tire rapidly when listening to a speaker who doesn't vary delivery style or a speaker who has a monotonous voice. A speaker's voice that is intelligible and of good quality may still not appeal to listeners. You may vary your voice and at the same time improve the communication by considering the vocal fundamentals of rate, volume, force, pitch, and emphasis. Thus variety is a spice of oratory.

- It is generally seen that many people speak at a rate of from 100 to 180 words a minute when presenting a talk. In normal speech, however, we vary the rate often so that even within the 100 to 180 word constraints there is much change. The temperamentally excitable person may speak at a rapid rate all the time, and the stolid person generally talks in a slow drawl. The enthusiastic but confident individual, however, will vary the rate of delivery to emphasize ideas and feelings. A slower rate may be appropriate for presenting main points, while a more rapid rate may lend itself to support material. The experienced speaker also knows that an occasional pause punctuates thought and emphasizes ideas. A dramatic pause at the proper time may express feelings and ideas even more effectively than words.
- Pitch or volume is important for any speaker. Always be certain that all the audience can hear you. Nothing hinders the effect of a talk more than to have some listeners unable to hear. On the other hand, the talk should not be too loud for a small room. A bombastic or overly loud speaker tires his audience or listeners very soon.
- Pitch is the highness or lowness of the voice. All things being equal, a higher pitched voice carries better than a low pitched one. On the other hand, listeners will tend to tire faster when listening to the higher pitched voice. If your voice is within normal limits—neither too high nor too low—work for variety as you speak.
- There may be use of force at times to emphasize and dramatize ideas. A drowsy audience will come to

attention quickly if the speaker uses force effectively. At times a sudden reduction in force may be as effective as a rapid increase. You can help to add emphasis and improve communication by learning to control the pitch and force of your tone of speaking.

- The greater or more sudden the change, the greater the emphasis will be. Emphasis obviously stems from all forms of vocal variety, and any change in rate, force, or pitch will influence the emphasis. As a speaker you will want to use emphasis wisely. Two things should be avoided: *over*emphasis and *continual* emphasis. Be judicious. Emphasizing a point beyond its real value may cause you to lose credibility with your listeners. So, take care while emphasing a point.

SINCERITY

A good speaker certainly needs to prepare well and possess strong delivery skills to do an effective job in front of a group. But something more is needed. To be really effective, a speaker must be sincere. So long as you obviously try to generate light and not merely heat, listeners will be amazingly tolerant of weaknesses in both preparation and delivery. But give them a chance to suspect your sincerity, and you lose effectiveness. And once lost, effectiveness is nearly impossible to regain. What is sincerity? Sincerity may be defined as a state of appearing to be without deceit, pretense, or hypocrisy—a state of honesty, truthfulness, and faithfulness. Sincerity toward your listeners is reflected in your eye contact, enthusiasm, and concern about audience members as individuals.

Sincerity toward the subject is judged by whether or not you seem involved and interested in the subject or topic of the talk. Sincerity toward self is displayed in the confidence and concern you have that you are doing the best job possible. Lack of sincerity in any of these areas will, hinder your communication directly.

□□

Chapter 10

Assertiveness and Negotiation

ASSERTIVENESS

Assertiveness is a trait taught by many personal development experts and psychotherapists and the subject of many popular self-help books. It is linked to self-esteem and considered an important communication skill.

As a communication style and strategy, assertiveness is distinguished from aggression and passivity. How people deal with personal boundaries; their own and those of other people, helps to distinguish between these three concepts. Passive communicators do not defend their own personal boundaries and thus allow aggressive people to harm or otherwise unduly influence them.

They are also typically not likely to risk trying to influence anyone else. Aggressive people do not respect the personal boundaries of others and thus are liable to harm others while trying to influence them. A person communicates assertively by not being afraid to speak his or her mind or trying to influence others, but doing so in a way that respects the personal boundaries of others. They are also willing to defend themselves against aggressive incursions.

Assertive style of behaviour is to interact with people while standing up for your rights. Being assertive is to one's benefit most of the time but it does not mean that one always gets what he/she wants. The result of being assertive is that:

- You feel good about yourself
- Other people know how to deal with you and there is nothing vague about dealing with you.

What Is Assertiveness?

Assertiveness is the ability to express yourself and your rights without violating the rights of others. It is appropriately direct, open, and honest communication which is self-enhancing and expressive. Acting assertively will allow you to feel self-confident and will generally gain you the respect of your peers and friends. It can increase your chances for honest relationships, and help you to feel better about yourself and your self-control in everyday situations. This, in turn, will improve your decision-making ability and possibly your chances of getting what you really want from life.

Assertiveness basically means the ability to express your thoughts and feelings in a way that clearly states your needs and keeps the lines of communication open with the other. However, before you can comfortably express your needs, you must believe you have a legitimate right to have those needs.

Assertiveness Techniques

Assertiveness training involves the learning of skills and techniques for resisting manipulation and coping with criticism. Two of the key assertive techniques are fogging and negative assertion.

- ***Fogging:*** Fogging requires some self-control, but it can be devastatingly effective. Imagine that one day, when you were out walking, a thick fog descended and left you unsure of which way to turn. You might feel frustrated or angry, but there'd be nothing you could do to the fog to relieve the frustration. Punching the fog, throwing missiles at it or cursing it would leave it unaffected. This explains the name of one of the key techniques taught in assertiveness training. This will have been discovered accidentally by many people who work in jobs that involve a lot of contact with the general public, many of whom must surely practice fogging regularly without being aware of the term.

Fogging involves training yourself to stay calm in the face of criticism, and agreeing with whatever may be fair and useful in it. By refusing to be provoked and upset by criticism, you remove its destructive power. Why, after all, should you crave someone else's complete approval, when doing so gives them power over you?

So, for instance, if someone calls you stupid, you can agree that sometimes you are. After all, everyone does foolish things sometimes. 'Stupid' is a relative term, and you probably *are* unintelligent if compared to, say, world renowned Professor Scientist Stephen Hawking. If someone criticizes your work, you can probably agree that it could be better. Even if it's already pretty good, there's likely to be some way in which you could make it better still.

The point of fogging is that it robs your critic's words of their destructive power. While superficially it may seem like a submissive strategy, it is in fact assertive because of what it implies. By refusing to become upset or angry in the face of criticism, you're denying your critic the satisfaction of seeing you being intimidated and disempowered. If they're just trying to bully you, and their words don't overpower you, there's a good chance that they'll turn their attentions to someone else who's easier to intimidate.

Phrases typically used when fogging include: 'That could be true', 'You're probably right'. 'Sometimes I think so myself', 'I agree', 'That's true', 'You're right' and 'You have a point there.' A phrase that is *never* used when fogging, but is constantly implied, is: 'So what?'

- ***Negative assertion:*** But what if the person who's complaining has valid, specific points to make about how you can improve? Well, then you can use negative assertion. This simply means agreeing with those parts of the criticism that are valid, but without allowing yourself to become consumed by guilt and self-loathing.

So if they tell you that your homework's late and it *is* late, admit it. Just say "Yes, you're right. I need to organize my time better' - or words to that effect. Then change your behaviour if you want to, or don't change if you don't want to - but either way, don't beat yourself up just because you've been criticized.

Another form of negative assertion simply owns up to your mistakes before anyone's even taken you to task for them: for instance, by turning up late at the office and simply saying "Hi, I'm late". In that situation, you are acknowledging that there's a problem and accepting responsibility for the situation, which should count in your favour with any bosses or colleagues who are annoyed with you.

Assertiveness training teaches that it's also important to acknowledge compliments, and accept them if you believe them to be sincere (rather than manipulative buttering-up) and agree with the nice things that are being said about you. The really important thing is that, at all times, you are the ultimate judge of your own behaviour.

What Does Assertive Communication Look Like?

Much of our communication is non-verbal. A person with an assertive communication style has a body language that conveys openness and receptiveness. Posture is upright, movements are fluid and relaxed, and tone of voice is clear and with inflection. An assertive person makes good eye contact, and is aware of personal space.

When giving opinions, an assertive person is willing to express his opinion, and also is open to hearing other's points of view. He is direct, but not argumentative or threatening. He does not use sarcasm or gossip as a way to communicate. He does not silently sit back out of fear of not being liked.

When an assertive person receives feedback from others, she is able to listen and accept what the other person has to say, even if she doesn't agree. Many people have a hard time receiving feedback, even if it's positive. How many times has someone paid you a compliment and you simply dismiss it, or minimize it rather than hearing it and simply saying "thanks"! No one likes to hear negative feedback, but an assertive person does not react to criticism by counter-attacking, denying, or feeling anxious or inadequate. He makes conscious choices about how to respond to the criticism.

He may ask for clarification to make sure he is really hearing what the other person is saying. He can validate the others' feelings, without necessarily agreeing with the person's feedback. If the negative feedback is valid, he accepts responsibility.

Strategies For Developing Assertive Communication

- Watch your body posture – practice using an open, assertive body language and voice.
- Think before you speak. Take a few seconds to make sure you are conveying the right message, and in the way you want to convey it.
- Don't apologize if it's not warranted.
- Remember it is ok to say "No".
- Remember everyone is entitled to an opinion, and don't try to convince others that yours is the "right" one. Also know that you don't have to apologize or make excuses.

Final Thoughts

- Be patient – learning new behaviours takes time, and it will feel awkward at first.
- Practice leads to improvement.
- Expect some resistance from others.
- Becoming assertive may never feel as comfortable as being passive or aggressive, if that's your learned style, but the rewards are worth the effort.
- Recognize and validate yourself for improvement.

NEGOTIATION

Negotiation is not the art of manipulating another person. Negotiation is a type of collaboration, even if you need to convince the other person that it is in their best interest to work together. Manipulation is forcing your goals and opinions on another person.

What is Negotiation?

Negotiating is simply "working with other to achieve some beneficial result." It is one of those skills that take a few hours to learn and a lifetime to master. It is not a genetic trait we're born with, like athletic or artistic ability. No matter what education level or social position, the negotiation skills are not beyond your capabilities. It just takes time, a little education, attention to honing our skills, and your life will be better.

Parts To Negotiation

There are three parts to negotiation: communication style, personality type and goals. Each of these elements need to be balanced between the two people negotiating before anyone can manipulate a desirable outcome.

- ***Communication Styles:*** A good communicator can identify a person's personality type and communication style. The communication style a negotiator uses does not necessarily match the audience's, but the audience will find it familiar and be comfortable using it. Some communication styles are directly to the point, void of facts. Others layout the facts, letting the audience come to their own opinion before the negotiator offers their opinion or goal. Using the wrong communication style can make the audience feel like they are being 'sold' or 'coerced'.
- ***Personality Type:*** The personality type determines what the audience considers a strong enough motivation to change their plans work with you. The negotiator will use the audience's values and goals to speak using a language, motives, goals, and values their audience will find appealing.

  The audience's personality type will also determine how long the presentation is, and what props the negotiator uses. An artistic person will like to see slides. A driver personality will want facts and figures they can take away with them.
- ***Goals:*** The expert negotiator does not focus on their goals, but the audience's goals. The art of negotiating is

making the audience believe that they are coming out on top of the agreement, without the negotiator begging or selling.

- Goals are often motivated by people's desire for relationships, building wealth, improving security, feeling good about yourself, and achieving a socially 'higher' goal. A negotiator will use these goals to 'speak' to the audience and help them reach their goals by reaching their own goals.

Objective

Negotiating is not a forceful encounter. Act collaboratively, not competitively. It is not "me against you". The other person is a bargaining partner. Everyone must come away with a benefit, or the party who has nothing to loose will leave. This is seen when a man falls in love. The court a woman until she marries him, treating her as the object of his love, instead of an equal partner who must continually be courted. This is also seen in business when one company merges with another, and then guts the minor company, leaving the remaining workers feeling wounded.

It is a big mistake to think you can use negotiations to get something for nothing. When negotiating, present your case as if both parties are on equal ground. Everyone can succeed at negotiating if they make "Mutual Benefit" their mantra.

Summary

There are many places to learn how to negotiate, about communication styles, and personality styles. Learning to listen can also give you an edge. Pro negotiators spend more time listening instead of talking. They do not cut-their-own-throats by cutting off the audience why their ideas and goals are wrong, or poorly motivated. They do not finish the audience's sentences. And, in the end, they earn the audience's trust, the first goal of any pro negotiator—Negotiation!

Negotiations Are Often Plagued By Misunderstanding

During a negotiation, communication often resembles the sending of smoke signals in a high wind. Difficulties with communicating pose a serious problem, since communication is the lifeblood of negotiations. Just as blood clots block circulation and cause heart attacks, poor communication blocks progress and ruptures negotiations and relationships.

- ***Cause:*** When we communicate, we focus on telling them what we think. We tend to focus on what we think we are saying rather than what the other party hears. The other party may not hear our message as we intend it, and we may not hear theirs'.
- ***Approach:*** Aim for two-way communication. Two-way communication means that both parties are listening as well as speaking. No message is truly communicated until it is heard and understood. Listening is among the most powerful things a negotiator can do. Listening provides information about interests, options, the relationship and areas for possible commitment. It demonstrates to others that we believe their views are worthy of careful consideration. If we can demonstrate to the other party that we have understood their views, it will be easier for them to listen to ours. Listening to and understanding the other side's point of view also enhances our ability to communicate with them in terms they will not misinterpret. Consequently, our proposals are likely to be more persuasive.

□□

Chapter 11

Preparing for Interview

People who consistently succeed at interviews are those who take the time to prepare their own answers rather than simply using answers they have read or heard elsewhere.

Whether you're a recent school leaver or a seasoned professional, you should know how to prepare highly effective answers and how to deliver them in a confident manner whilst establishing that all-important rapport with interviewers. One of the major obstacles to successful interviewing is organising a vast amount of detail about what you've done in previous jobs (or at school or university) and expressing this information in a clear and convincing way at the interview. It is necessary to prevent yourself from:

- Giving those long-winded answers that drive interviewers to distraction;
- Failing to mention important key achievements and kicking yourself afterwards;
- Being stumped by certain questions and not providing an intelligent response;
- Failing to build rapport and trust.

The reason for this is simple: if you fail to establish rapport and trust, it is highly unlikely that you will get the job—no matter how technically brilliant your answers are.

The skills and techniques you will develop from reading this book will remain with you for the rest of your working life. They will immeasurably improve your chances of winning those hard-to-get jobs and contribute to a rewarding career.

INTERVIEW MYTHS

One important reason people fail at interviews is because of several misconceptions, or myths, about what really happens during the course of an interview. All of us know that the purpose of interviews is for an interviewer to hire someone who will perform well in a particular job, but beyond that few people fully grasp how interviews really work and what makes one candidate stand out more than another. This lack of understanding represents a major obstacle to maximising performance when sitting before an interviewer and trying to give your best answers. Interviews are no different to other endeavors in life: the better you understand how they work (or don't work), the higher the probability of tackling them successfully. An understanding of the underlying dynamics inherent in most interviews is an important start to improving your interview performance.

Myth No. 1: The Best Person For The Job Gets It

Sometimes this is true—especially in a situation where everyone knows everyone else, such as when a company is recruiting internally. However, this is often not the case. In order for the best person for the job to win it, a number of very important things need to be in place (and even then, there's no guarantee). These include:

- The interviewer knows what questions to ask and how to search for the truthfulness in answers. These two things may sound simple enough, but a large proportion of people conducting interviews may not have received training, they lack interview experience and often do not even go to the trouble of preparing for the interview.
- The interviewer is not taken in by the charm, good looks, great humour or any other aspect of the interviewee. This can be a difficult obstacle, even for experienced interviewers.

- The interviewee has learned how to clearly articulate their skills, key achievements and how they can add value to the organisation.
- There is no personality clash between interviewer and interviewee.
- Neither party is having a bad day.

In an ideal world, the best person for the job would always win it; however, the reality is that it is often the person who performs best at the interview who wins the prize. Some employers—usually the ones who have been badly burnt by hiring the wrong people in the past—go to great lengths to set up professional hiring procedures designed to minimise hiring mistakes. Whilst some of these procedures are effective in improving candidate selection, they do not guarantee that the best person for the job will actually win it. In the final analysis, choosing someone for a job involves at least one human being making a decision about another, and no matter what we do to eliminate subjectivity, as human beings it is impossible to put aside our predispositions, predilections and personal preferences—no matter how much we may try to. The important lessons here are:

- Don't automatically pull out of applying for a job if you know someone better suited for the job is also applying for it. If you go to the trouble of preparing properly for the interview, there's a good chance that you may be seen as the preferred candidate— especially if the other person takes the interview for granted and fails to prepare.
- If you happen to know that you're the best person for the job, avoid taking the interview for granted. Behave as though you're competing against formidable rivals. Take the time to prepare properly. Just because you've got a lot of experience does not mean you know how to convey this message at an interview.

Myth No. 2: Interviews Are Like School Exams—The More You Say, The Better You'll Do

Yes, interviews are a bit like exams in so far as that you're asked a number of questions to which you need to respond intelligently, but there the similarities end. Unlike exams, where lots of accurate detail is important, interviews are more about interacting and rapport building whilst simultaneously articulating smart answers. And a smart answer is often not the most detailed. In fact, long and overly detailed answers can drive interviewers to distraction, despite their technical accuracy. Knowing when to stop talking is a skill all successful interviewees have. Also unlike many exams, there are often no right or wrong answers in interviews. We're all different and come to interviews from different backgrounds and business sitations. What is important at an interview is to justify your actions and talk about your achievements in a confident manner.

Myth No. 3: Interviewers Know What They're doing

Some interviewers are very good at what they do, especially fulltime professionals (provided they're not suffering from interview fatigue). However, many managers and owners of small businesses often flounder because interviewing is not something they do on a regular basis. Some sure signs of a bad interviewer are:

- *They* do most of the talking.
- They sound as though they've made up their mind about you in the first five minutes.
- They seem to pluck their questions randomly out of the ether.
- Their phone keeps ringing and they answer it.
- They sound like very sharp and less-than-honest salespeople when it comes to selling the job.

Some sure signs of a good interviewer are:

- They have their questions carefully prepared in advance.
- They want to know what you've done and how you've done it, including specific examples.
- They let *you* do most of the talking.
- They may want to interview you more than once.
- They will try to make you feel at ease.
- They are genuinely interested in your accomplishments, skills and the type of person you are.

Inexperienced interviewers generally don't ask the right questions and can easily be swayed by factors that have little to do with your ability to perform in the job. So if you are being interviewed by an inexperienced interviewer, don't wait to be asked a good question— one that will allow you to talk about all your wonderful skills and qualities. Rather, take the initiative in as unobtrusive a way as possible and talk about the things you feel the interviewer might really want to know. Unfortunately, this may not always be possible—especially if you're being interviewed by a forceful personality who loves the sound of his own voice. If ever you find yourself in such a situation, don't panic. Remind yourself that interviews are just as much about rapport-building as they are about answering questions. So nod your head, smile and make all the right noises—talkative interviewers love people who agree with them.

Myth No. 4: Never Say 'I Don't Know'

Interviews are about making a positive impression by answering questions intelligently and building rapport with the interviewer. To this end, many interviewees feel that they have to provide the perfect answer to every question put to them, irrespective of whether or not they actually *know* the answer. Clearly, a great interview is one in which you can answer all the questions (and you should be able to do so if you take the time to prepare correctly); however, if you don't know the answer to something, it is better to admit to it rather than pretend to know and start waffling. Most interviewers can pick waffling a mile away and they don't like it for a couple of very important reasons: first, it is likely to make you sound dishonest; and second, it will make you sound considerably less than intelligent. You may as well not attend the interview if you give the impression that you're neither honest nor bright.

Trying to answer a question that you have little idea about could undermine an otherwise great interview. This does not mean that you cannot attempt answers that you are unsure of. There's nothing wrong with having a go, as long as you make your uncertainty clear to the interviewer at the outset. Here's what an answer may sound like:

"I have to be honest and say that this is not an area I'm familiar with, though I am very interested in it. If you like, I'm happy to have a go at trying to address the issue, as long as you're not expecting the perfect answer."

OR

"I'd love to answer that question, but I need to be honest upfront and say that this is not an area that I'm overly familiar with, though I'm very interested in increasing my knowledge about it."

Myth No. 5: Good-looking People Get The Job

If the job is for a drop-dead gorgeous femme fatale type in a movie, then good looks would certainly help, but for most other jobs the way you look is not as big a deal as many people make out. As we've already discussed, there will always be an inexperienced employer who will hire on the basis of superficial factors, but most employers are smarter than that. The claim that good-looking people get the job over plain-looking people makes one seriously flawed assumption—that employers make a habit of putting someone's good looks before the interests of their livelihood. On the contrary, most businesses find themselves in highly competitive environments and employers are only too keenly aware that a poor hiring decision can prove very costly.

This is not to say that appearance and a bright personality are not important factors at an interview. It is very important that you dress appropriately and try your best to demonstrate all your friendly qualities. Good looks are certainly overrated in interviews, but an appropriate appearance and a friendly personality are not.

Myth No. 6: If you Answer The Questions Better Than The Others, You'll Get The Job

Being able to articulate good answers in an interview is very important, and failure to do so will almost certainly mean you don't get the job. However, interviews—are much more than just giving good answers. They're also about convincing the interviewer that you will be a nice person to work with. To put it another way, it doesn't matter how good your answers are technically, if the interviewer doesn't like you there's not much chance you'll get the job (unless your talents are unique, extremely difficult to find or the interviewer is desperate).

So avoid thinking about interviews just in terms of answering questions correctly. Interviews are also about establishing rapport and trust, and whilst there is no fail-safe method in doing this, there are things you can do (and things you should not do) that will go a long way towards improving your skills in this all-important area of interviewing.

Myth No. 7: You Should Try To Give The Perfect Answer

Many people stumble over their words, repeat themselves and talk in circles because they're trying to articulate the perfect answer—or what they *think* constitutes the perfect answer. Some people are so obsessed with delivering the perfect answer that they don't stop until they produce what in their opinion is a word perfect response.

Because we can never be entirely sure of what the interviewer wants to hear, some of us will keep on talking in the hope that we'll cover all bases. The problem with this approach is that we end up talking *too* much, leading to the interviewer losing concentration— which, of course, is the last thing you need at an interview. The reality is that in most cases there is no such thing as the perfect answer. The lesson here is: it makes a lot of sense to settle for a good answer that gets to the point rather than meander all over the place searching for the elusive perfect answer.

Myth No. 8: You Must Ask Questions To Demonstrate Your Interest And Intelligence

Many interviewees are under the mistaken belief that they must ask questions at the end of the interview. There seems to be a common belief amongst many interviewees that this makes them sound more intelligent as well as more interested in the job. This is not true. Asking questions simply for the sake of doing so won't improve your chances of getting a job. It could even make you sound a little dull—especially if you ask questions about matters that were already covered during the course of the interview.

Only ask a question if you have a genuine query. Acceptable questions include those relating directly to the job you're applying for, as well as working conditions and company policies on such things as on pay, leave, and so on. Interviewers never mind answering questions about such matters, but they do mind answering questions they perceive to be irrelevant. If you have no questions to ask, simply say something like: "Thank you, but I have no questions. You've been very thorough during the course of the interview and have covered all the important matters regarding the job". There's nothing wrong with including a compliment to the interviewer about their thoroughness and professionalism—provided it doesn't go over the top or sound like grovelling.

Two further points need to be made about asking questions. First, avoid asking too many questions. On the whole, interviewers do not enjoy role reversals. Second, never ask potentially embarrassing questions. These can include:

- A question relating to a negative incident;
- Something that's not supposed to be in the public domain;
- A difficult question that may stump the interviewer.

The rule of thumb is: if you think a question may cause embarrassment, err on the side of caution and avoid it.

Myth No. 9: Relax And Just Be Yourself

Whilst it is important to be relaxed and show your better side, it is also very important to understand that interviews are not social engagements. Most interviews are highly formalised events in which otherwise innocuous behaviours are deemed unacceptable. In short, being your usual self could spell disaster (as contradictory as that may sound). For instance, if being yourself means leaning back on your chair, dressing somewhat shabbily and making jokes, you might find yourself attending an inordinate number of interviews. Whilst interviewers like people to be relaxed, they also have definite expectations about what behaviours are appropriate for an interview— and you violate these expectations at your peril!

Myth No. 10: Interviewers Are Looking For Flaws

The danger with this myth is that it can easily lead to interviewees adopting a defensive, perhaps even distrustful, attitude during the interview. If you believe that the interviewer is assiduously searching for your flaws, it will more than likely undermine your attempts to establish that all-important rapport and trust. It may also prevent you from opening up and giving really good answers. Rest assured that most interviewers do not prepare their interview questions with a view to uncovering your flaws. Questions are mostly prepared with a view to giving the interviewer an overall or holistic insight into what you have to offer the company. A good interviewer will indeed uncover areas in which you are not strong, but that is a far cry from thinking that the interviewer is hell bent on uncovering only your flaws.

It is very important to treat every question as an opportunity to excel rather than being unnecessarily guarded. It is only by answering the questions that you can demonstrate how good you are. To treat questions as objects of suspicion makes no sense at all.

Understanding the myths surrounding interviews gives you a great start for success. Remember, interviews are no different to other endeavors in life: the better you understand their underlying nature the higher the probability you'll tackle them successfully. An insight into common interview myths will arm you with the information you need to prevent you from falling into those disheartening traps. Just as importantly, a clearer picture of the true nature of interviews better informs the rest of your preparation and will contribute to your confidence and performance.

Summary Of Key Points

The best person for the job does not necessarily win it—often it's the person who gives the best interview.

- Interviews are more than just giving technically correct answers. They're also very much about building rapport.
- Not all interviewers know what they're doing; your job is to know how to handle the good and bad interviewer.
- It's better to be honest and admit ignorance than try to pretend you know an answer and come across as disingenuous and less than bright.
- Good looking people win jobs—may be in movies, but on the whole, employers are keen to hire talent over superficial factors.
- Striving to give the perfect answer can get you into trouble. It's better to give a good answer that's to the point rather than searching for perfection; besides, often there's no such thing as the perfect answer.
- Do not ask questions for the sake of it. Only ask a question if you have a genuine query that has not been covered.
- Interviews are formal occasions requiring relatively formal behaviours. Interviewers will expect this and may react negatively if they don't see it.
- Interviewers do not spend all their time looking for your flaws. They're more interested in getting an overall picture of who you are. Avoid answering questions defensively. It's much better to see every question as an opportunity to highlight your best points.

CONVINCING THEM YOU'RE RIGHT FOR THE JOB

Doing well at interviews is not nearly as difficult as many people think. With correct preparation and a little practice, most people who dread interviews can learn to excel. The important thing to note is that performing well at interviews is a *learned* process. Highly effective interviewees are not born with interview skills; rather, they teach themselves what to say, how to say it and how to behave during an interview.

COMMON INTERVIEW MISTAKES

All of us have made mistakes during interviews, and most of us have walked out of interviews thinking of all the great things we forgot to mention and all the things we shouldn't have said. But the most important thing about mistakes is learning from them—and not repeating them. Here are some common interview mistakes:

Failing To Express Oneself Clearly

Often, because of anxiety and wanting to say things perfectly, we try too hard and turn what should be simple sentences into convoluted nonsense. Simple language is always the most effective. Avoid trying to sound knowledgeable by using jargon or complex sentences.

Not Being Aware Of One's Body Language

Many interviewees succeed in alienating the interviewer because they pay little or no attention to their body language. Body language is an extremely powerful communicator, and failing to use it effectively will almost certainly put you at a significant disadvantage. Eye contact, sitting position and facial expressions are all very important aspects of interviewing, and need to be thought through before the interview.

Failing To Control Those Nerves

Sometimes people allow their nerves to get so out of control that they fail to establish rapport and even forget their answers. Feeling anxious before and during an interview is common. In fact, a touch of nerves can be a good thing. But there is no need to be the victim of debilitating nerves.

Failing To Give Appropriate Examples

Failing to give examples, or giving inappropriate examples, will spell disaster. Before the interview, it is important to think of relevant examples of what you've achieved and how you went about realising those achievements.

Saying that you achieved something without being able to back it up with specific examples will only get you a rejection letter. Your examples need to be easy to understand, follow a logical sequence and be relevant to the needs of the employer. None of this happens without preparation.

Trying Too Hard To Please The Interviewer

Whilst building rapport and trust during the interview is critical, few interviewers appreciate interviewees going overboard with their behaviour. Obsequious behaviours are generally seen as a form of deceit and carry little weight—in fact, they can undermine your efforts to create trust.

THERE'S NOTHING WRONG WITH YOU

You've probably committed at least some of the mistakes. It's very important to realise that making such mistakes is common. In other words, *there's nothing wrong with you.* In the vast majority of cases, performing poorly at an interview happens because of the very nature of interviews—it's the interview process that is the culprit. So an awareness of the basic nature of interviews is the first step in a step-by-step process by which you can significantly improve your performance. A great place to start is to ask: 'What does it take to convince the interviewer that you're the best person for the job?'The answer to this question can best be summarised in four parts:

- Correct preparation
- Knowing the things that are important to interviewers
- Practising your answers
- Perseverance

Correct Preparation

How well you perform at an interview will largely depend on how well you have prepared for it. Failure to correctly prepare almost certainly means you will not perform at your best. In some cases, it will mean performing quite badly, which may contribute to the erosion of your confidence. Even if you're lucky enough to be the favoured candidate, and are almost certain to win the position by just turning up, you should still take the time to prepare because the better you perform, the greater the likelihood that you will negotiate a better salary—and often the difference in money can be substantial. We've all heard people boast that they've never prepared for an interview in their lives and have done all right. Whilst this boast may not be an idle one, closer inspection will usually reveal that these people were:

- Lucky—that is, in the right place at the right time.
- Well connected.
- Working in a favourable labour market where there was a huge demand for employees coupled with low supply.
- Applying for jobs well within their comfort zone—that is, not stretching themselves to improve their position.

OR

- Applying for jobs internally and competing mainly against external candidates.

The Case For Preparation

To get prepared for an ensuing interview is necessrary. So an argument for interview preparation becomes compelling when you give some thought to the basic nature of interviews. Not only are you expected to sell yourself in a competitive environment, but you're also expected to compress large and often complex pieces of information into neat and highly articulate answers that avoid any negative connotations and contain the information the interviewer wants to hear. It's no wonder people's stress levels increase. But it doesn't end there. There are three additional reasons that make the case for interview preparation even more compelling:

- In most interviews, coming second isn't good enough. It's not just a matter of performing well; it's also a matter of beating everyone else.
- Many people find it very difficult to sell themselves at interviews because they've been conditioned by family and society not to blow their own trumpet. Making simple statements such as "I am very good at selling xyz" can be quite an obstacle to overcome.
- Interviews are rare events, thus making them unfamiliar and awkward.

It is unimaginable that you would fail to prepare for an event that is infrequent, competitive and requires behaviours not normally used. Yet that is exactly what people do when they walk into an interview without preparation.

There are two significant benefits in knowing that interviewers are keenly interested in basic generic questions, and that the vast majority of questions they can ask fall under one or more of these categories.

First, it guides you in the preparation of your answers. Rather than spending lots of time wading through randomly selected questions in the hope that you will have prepared the right answers, an understanding of the significance of the three key generic questions provides a direction and platform for your preparation. In short, you are able to plan your preparation around the following issues:

- Your skills, knowledge, experience key achievements and potential performance—*can you do the job?;*
- Your personal attributes—*are you the sort of person they can work with?;*
- Your motivation levels—*how motivated are you*?

Second, it provides a useful way to deal with questions at the actual interview. By sorting interview questions into one or more of the three generic question categories, your answers will gain added structure and a clearer direction simply because you know what the underlying purpose of the questions is. By learning how to recognise the real intent of a question, you minimise your chances of giving the wrong answer and/or waffling.

Practice

The third aspect of convincing an interviewer that you're the best person for the job is practice. Unfortunately, there are no shortcuts to developing great interview skills. Once you've prepared your answers, you need to sit down and practise them as much as you can. The more you practise, the better you'll be. How you practise is up to you. Do it in front of the mirror, sitting on your couch, pacing your room or while driving your car—but avoid practising in front of your boss!

- ***Practising Your Answers Aloud:*** It is important to practise your answers aloud, rather than just mentally rehearsing them. That's because the human brain distinguishes between talking and thinking and you need to stimulate the talking part of your brain. Thinking your answers at an interview will get you nowhere, unless the interviewer is a mind reader.

- ***Get Some Feedback:*** Ideally, you should do your practising at real interviews. The more interviews you attend, the better—even if you have to attend interviews for jobs that you're not really interested in. After the interview—assuming you're not the winning candidate—ring back the interviewer and ask for feedback on your performance. Some interviewers are happy to provide this feedback; however, many prefer not to because they find it threatening and a waste of their time. These people will either avoid you altogether or provide you with such watered-down feedback that it will be virtually useless.

  In some instances you may not be able to resolve this problem; however, you can increase your chances of getting honest feedback by making interviewers feel as comfortable as possible. You can do this by (*a*) assuring them that you only want five minutes of their time; and (*b*) telling them that the only reason you're seeking feedback is to improve future interview performance.

- ***Mock Interviews:*** If you cannot get yourself to as many interviews as you would like, it's a good idea to set up mock interviews with someone you can work with. The more closely you can simulate a real-life situation, more benefit you will derive. An effective way to conduct mock interviews is to get into role and stay in it for the entire interview.

  No distractions, no small talk and especially no starting again. If possible, avoid providing the questions to your helpers—let them come up with their own. If your helpers are not in a position to do this, give them lots of questions and ask them to choose the ones they want. The important thing for you is to get yourself used to answering *unexpected* questions. Furthermore, if you feel your helper can provide you with *honest* feedback on your performance, do not shy away from asking. You never know what you may learn. Often it's the small things that make a big difference. But be on your guard for overly positive feedback. Chances are that your helper will be a friend, and friends are well known for avoiding negatives.

Perseverance

The worst thing you can do when setting out to improve your interview performance is give up because it all seems too hard. Quitters invariably get nowhere. They certainly don't land great jobs and build great careers. On the other hand, people who persevere very often gain valuable insights simply because they have the stamina to stick it out. Remember the old saying 'success is one part talent and nine parts perseverance'.

The people we admire most are often those who face seemingly insurmountable obstacles yet instead of quitting, quietly resolve to overcome them. On the other side of the coin, the people we generally least respect are those who are forever starting things without finishing them. They tend to be the same people who make grandiose claims but end up delivering little or nothing.

One common characteristic that chronic quitters tend to have is low self-esteem— they don't really believe in themselves. And if you don't believe in yourself, others usually don't believe in you either—not a great place to be when you're trying to convince interviewers to believe in your abilities. These are the people who are often heard saying things such as: 'That's too hard', 'I can't learn that', 'What will others think', etc. They also tend to be the people who are always complaining about things but never seem to take any action to correct them because there's always an excuse.

You don't have to be a chronic quitter or burdened with low self-esteem to give up on working on your interview skills—there could be any number of other reasons. If you feel you might be one of those people who is standing on the precipice of quitting, here is a little exercise that can assist you to take a step or two back from the edge.

Suggested Activity: Neurolinguistic Programming: Based on neurolinguistic programming (NLP), this exercise is designed to influence how you feel. People often quit because they associate negative feelings with what they're doing. People who persevere have the power to feel good about their actions no matter how tedious or unconstructive these actions may seem to others. If you can make yourself feel good about the process of improving your interview skills, then there's a good chance that quitting will be the last thing on your mind. Next time you feel like quitting, you might like to find a quiet spot and take the following steps:

- Close your eyes and imagine yourself performing extremely well in an interview. Take your time to view this picture in as much detail as you can. Picture the faces of the enthusiastic interviewers, noticing how attentive they are and how impressed they are with your responses. Immerse yourself in the experience. Pay attention to the details, including sounds, smells, colours, temperature, and so on. Above all, capture the feeling of being successful. Do not hold yourself back. The better you make yourself feel, the more powerful the exercise will be.
- Keep on repeating this exercise until you capture that feeling of excitement. You may be able to generate greater excitement by picturing yourself in your new job. Imagine how good it is going to feel winning a great job. Imagine getting that all important phone call informing you of your success. Picture yourself in the position doing all those things you've dreamt of doing. The key to this exercise is to generate the great feeling that goes with succeeding at an interview. Your only limitation is your imagination.
- Once you've captured that feeling, the next step is to recreate it when you need it—in other words, when you feel like quitting. An effective way of recreating the

feeling of excitement is by installing what NLP refers to as an *anchor*. An anchor is a stimulus that triggers the desired feelings when you want them. An anchor can be something you do, say or imagine. Action anchors usually work best. For instance, you might cross your fingers or jump up in the air or pull your ears. It doesn't matter what it is, as long as you can do it easily when you want to and trigger the desired feelings. Every time you're afflicted with the scourge of quitting, use your anchor and let your ability to influence your feelings do the rest.

Summary Of Key Points

- Because of their nature, interviews are inherently challenging. Making mistakes at an interview is something that everyone does. The good news is that we can overcome our errors by correct preparation, practice and perseverance.
- Beware of faulty preparation. Avoid rote learning of other people's answers. Always prepare your own.
- Knowing what employers want to hear at an interview constitutes a great start for preparing your own answers and simplifies interview preparation. What most employers want to hear can be represented by three key questions:
  - — Can you do the job?
  - — Are you the sort of person they can work with?
  - — How motivated are you?
- Get in as much practice as you can and always ask for *honest* feedback.
- Perseverance is everything.
- Banish all thoughts of quitting by teaching yourself to associate strong feelings of excitement with improving your interview skills.

WHAT YOU MUST KNOW AND DO

Before an employer decides to give someone a job, they need

to be convinced that the person can either do the job properly or learn it quickly. It comes as no surprise to learn therefore that 'Can you do the job?' questions are the most common. They're also the ones people spend most time preparing for.

'Can You Do The Job?' Questions Include:

- Can you give us an example of a time you had to communicate something that was complex and controversial? How did you go about it?
- Tell us about one of your key achievements?
- An irate client rings and gives you a blast over the phone. How do you handle it?
- What do you think you can bring to this position?
- Can you give us an example of a project that you had to plan and organise? What steps did you take?
- How would you describe yourself? (At first glance this may not strike you as a 'Can you do the job?' question, but effective interviewees always look for ways to highlight their skills.)
- What would you say makes an effective manager of people?
- Why should we employ you?
- What do you regard as your greatest strength?
- The most important duty in your job will be to look after the x, y and z. Tell us how you intend going about it.

Unless you're being interviewed for a job that's almost identical to one you've already had, it is likely that you will be asked three types of 'Can you do the job?' questions. These are:

- Questions about duties that you have performed before;
- Questions about duties that you have not performed but whose skills you have mastered;
- Questions about duties that are entirely new to you.

Finding Out As Much About The Job As Possible

The first thing you need to do is take a very close look at the duties and requirements of the job you're applying for. It is these duties and requirements that will form the basis of your answers. There are several ways of collecting this sort of information:

- Scrutinising the job advertisement;
- Accessing a duty statement—if there is one;
- Contacting the employer or recruitment agent to clarify the main responsibilities of the job.

It is critical that you find out as much about the job as possible before sitting down and thinking about your answers. The best source of information is either the employer or the recruitment agent. Job ads and duty statements are useful (sometimes they're all that you will have); however, duty statements can often be out of date and job ads can lack sufficient information. Duty statements are simply a summary of the main duties of a job.

Talking to the right people can provide you with insights that often cannot be picked up from the written word. You might find out, for instance, that the position you're applying for was made vacant because the previous incumbent had poor interpersonal communication skills and became aggressive when anyone expressed a differing opinion. In such a case, it is likely that the employer will be looking for a replacement with excellent interpersonal communication and team player skills. You'd have a far better chance of winning the job if you had accessed this information before the interview and taken the time to prepare your answers.

Talking To An Employer To Find Out More

If you're able to talk to the employer, before the interview *be sure you've got your questions prepared.* The last thing you want to do is waste their time by stumbling through poorly thought-out questions. Here are some useful rules when talking to an employer before the interview:

- Avoid small talk and get straight to the point. Small talk will be seen as sucking up—which, of course, it is!
- Avoid asking too many questions—just ask the important ones, unless the employer has made it obvious

that they've got lots of time on their hands and is willing to talk to you.

- Never ask frivolous questions—those that can be answered from the advertisement or that a good applicant would be expected to know the answers to.
- Where necessary, provide a succinct reason why you're asking the question—the employer may not understand the significance of the question and could draw the wrong conclusions.
- Thank them for their time and tell them you're looking forward to the interview.

Gleaning Information From A Job Advertisement

When you scrutinise the job advertisement, make a list of all the duties/requirements associated with the position. The idea is to try to read between the lines as much as possible. The more duties and requirements you come up with, the more thorough your preparation will be, which will lessen the chances of being caught unprepared at the interview.

Steps to Interview Success

The four steps to interview success are designed to capture all the relevant information you need to construct interview answers within a simple-to-manage framework.

Most importantly, it's *your relevant* information, not information gathered from other people's answers you've read elsewhere. Once you've captured the required information, your next step is to put it together in response to a range of likely interview questions and then practise your answers.

One of the key advantages of the four steps method is that it lends itself to addressing a popular questioning technique commonly referred to as *behavioural questioning*. You can recognise one of these questions every time an interviewer asks you for specific examples to back up a claim you have made, including the steps you took and the obstacles you encountered. Behavioural questions are designed to uncover the actions (behaviours) behind an outcome or a duty.

If you're a graduate or a new entrant to the workforce, there's still a good chance that you will be asked behavioural questions; however, they will be limited in scope. Instead of asking for employment-related experience, interviewers will ask for study-or life-related incidences. For instance, interviewer may want to know how well you function in a team, so may ask you about the last time you had to complete an assignment with a group of students. The same principle applies to communication skills, planning and organising, conflict resolution, your ability to cope with change, and so on.

Once you've come up with as much information as you can about the job, you need to start thinking about preparing your answers regarding duties you've performed before. All you need to do is recount your past actions and achievements and link them to the new job.

But be careful not to take these interviews for granted. It is all too easy to fall into the trap of not preparing because you think that the questions will be easy. However, just because you've performed the same duties does not mean you will be able to articulate the details of what you did and how you did it. There's a big difference between doing something and actually having to talk about it in a succinct and coherent fashion.

The four Steps you need to follow are:

- *What I Did And How I Did It?* Make a list of all the duties and their requirements that you've successfully accomplished in the post.
- *How Long Should My Answers Be?* It all depends on the question and the circumstances.

  It is reasonable to assume that the interviewer may want to spend more time on particular questions. If you've done your homework, there's a good chance that you'll know beforehand which questions the interviewers will wish to spend a little extra time on. If not, it's up to you to be as alert as possible during the interview. Look out for any clues (such as body language and tone of voice) that may indicate the interviewer is placing extra importance on particular questions. The point is that it's

OK to spend a little extra time on these sorts of questions.

Avoid subjective or liberal interpretations of questions. Listen very carefully to the question, and *answer it*. This sounds obvious, but people do have a bad habit of assuming that the interviewer is wanting to hear a whole lot of other things. Just stick to the question. If interviewers have other questions, there's a good chance they'll ask them.

- *Context Or Situation In Which I Did It?:* Without context, your answers will sound empty or only half-completed. In fact, it is often a good idea to *begin your answers* by giving the interviewer an insight into the context in which you performed the duties.

  Please note that you only need to establish context once for each job you did. Repeating context for the same job is nonsensical and is likely to make the interviewer think that you bumped your head against something hard on your way to the interview!

- *Outcomes:* This step involves writing down the key outcomes or results of your actions. Outcomes or achievements are arguably the most important aspect of your work. There's little point in doing all the right things if you don't achieve any positive outcomes. From an interviewer's point of view, outcomes are critical.When thinking about outcomes, it is useful to separate them into *organisation* and *personal* categories.

  Organisational outcomes include any improvements accrued by the organisation as a result of your work. Saying you implemented a new filing system is great, but your answer would be much better if you also articulated the benefit of this new filing system to the employer. For instance:

  – Productivity rose by 5 per cent.
  – Quality of service, as measured by customer feedback, improved significantly.

- Customer service levels improved by 12 per cent.
- Staff satisfaction and moral improved by over 8 per cent.
- Turn-around times nearly halved.
- 'Best guess' estimates are fine in this situation.

Articulating personal outcomes can be a very effective interview technique, particularly when those outcomes are directly relevant to the job you're applying for. It's also an effective way to highlight an important skill or insight to an interviewer who seems to be incapable of asking appropriate questions.

Personal outcomes include any benefits *you* have accrued as a result of your work. These can include:

- Learning new skills;
- Improving existing skills;
- Gaining new insights;
- Various forms of recognition, including promotion or monetary gain.

Pose Your Own Questions

Generating your own questions is a simple process if you tackle it from the perspective of the interviewer. Put yourself in the shoes of the interviewer and ask yourself what questions you would need to ask to ascertain whether the interviewee could perform the relevant duty or job requirement. You will need to take into account behavioural questioning techniques, which are designed to uncover the specific actions behind stated claims. An example of a behavioural based question relating to working in an entrepreneurial environment is: 'Tell us about the way you dealt with working in a fast-paced entrepreneurial environment. What steps or techniques worked for you?' Notice the key phrases: 'the way you dealt with' and 'What steps or techniques worked for you?' This question is trying to uncover the key behaviours underpinning successful work in an entrepreneurial environment.

By asking yourself such questions, there is a good chance that you will come close to anticipating the interview questions—or at least be more precise about the intent of the interview questions. The actual question at the interview probably will sound different to the question you posed yourself, but its intent or purpose will be similar. In other words, even though questions may be worded differently, the content of your answers should be relevant to the interview.

Where possible begin your answer with the context. Think of context as the foundation upon which you build some of your answers. The clearer the context, the more sense the rest of your answer will make to the interviewer. The interviewer will know what sort of environment you were working in and how important your duties were to the success of the job, not to mention your own employment.

Once you've established context in one question you do not have to keep on mentioning the same context for every question relating to the same workplace. Only mention context again if a new one is being discussed.

A good interview answer will generally contain the following points:

- A context;
- Specific examples;
- What you did and how you did it;
- Outcomes;
- It will get directly to the point.

FACE THE INTERVIEW: BE PREPARED

Ever wondered what it would be like to face an interview for the first time?

Confidence and *being calm* is the main mantra in facing an interview and you're sure to be at ease from thereon.

The word "interview" gets you nervous and makes you go weak in the knees. Many companies and classifieds today use the phrase "formal talk" in place of an interview. Even though the phrase says formal, it somehow portrays more of an informal meeting. This makes the candidate or the interviewee relax and prepare well beforehand.

The interviewer belongs to the HR department of his/her company. They are given the responsibility of employing individuals based on various criteria. The interviewer or the employer will always act in authority and will take the opportunity to test you in every possible way. After all, it is a job, a duty and a responsibility that will be handed over to you. Depending on the experience and skills required to employ individuals, the employer will test you for the concerned job opening.

Depending on the company and job opening, many a times, interviews are solely an alternative for a personality test. Industrial psychologists or a qualified counsellor usually conducts these. These tests study the capability of the individual on various factors like level of motivation, interest, positive outlook and reliability. Once the candidate clears this test, he/she is then sent to the HR department for screening for the job opening.

The employer is mainly looking for the 3 C's in an employee-*Credibility, Confidence and Capability*. You will be tested on various skills and usually asked questions that will give an insight into your personality and attitude. The employer will brief you on the company, its strength, achievements and goals.

Your personality, enthusiasm, communication skills, interpersonal skills and confidence are the keys to impressing your employer.

The famous saying, "*the first impression is the last impression*" holds true even for an employer-candidate acquaintance. It works both ways - the impression you create will have an effect on the questions asked and your likeability factor. Likewise the impression you have of him/her will affect the interview process, your understanding of the company and work atmosphere.

Do a bit of pre-research on the company, its employees, its work and especially the job opening that you have applied for. You should have a thorough understanding of the requirements of the position. Your research will help you communicate your interests for the job and your background to the employer and will facilitate a successful interview.

Tips at a Glance

- Make sure that you get there a little earlier than the scheduled time.
- Dress appropriately and look confident. Your appearance will leave a lasting impression on the employer.
- During the interview do not look nervous. Keep a check on your non-verbal behaviour too. Give thoughtful answers to all the questions that the interviewer asks you. Speak clearly and be professional in your speech. Your answers must be precise and to the point.
- You will usually be asked to talk a little about yourself, your background and work experience. Be concise and use examples if needed. A little touch of humour does help.
- The goal is to show the employer your interest in the job and their company and that your skills and enthusiasm can help the company.

Towards the end of the interview the employer will ask you if you have any questions. Do not forego this opportunity. This will give the employer an impression of your interest in the job. Ask your concerns but be careful not to ask too many questions. Interviews are always time limited.

Finally, and most importantly, remember the 3 C's, relax and stay calm through the interview process.

□□

Chapter 12

Communication in Groups

COMMUNICATION SKILLS FOR GROUP

This is understandable in light of the fact that decision making is an activity in which individuals and groups engage numerous times virtually every day. Of the many topics on which communication scholars interested in the study of groups have focused, none has been the object of more sustained attention than that of decision making. It is even more understandable when one considers the significant ramifications such activity often has for the decision makers and others' well-being. At an individual level, the activity is exclusively cognitive, unless, of course, one solicits input from others while attempting to reach a decision. In groups, the process of making decisions is manifested and unfolds in the communicative exchanges that occur among the members.

In either case, the likelihood of choosing appropriately depends on a number of skills. This book identifies such skills and relates them to the outcomes that decision-making groups achieve. The term *skill,* refers to a capacity, either mental or behavioural in nature, that, in structured form, enables one to perform tasks necessary for the production of particular outcomes.

Skills can be genetic in origin or acquired. In both instances, they fall along a continuum from undeveloped to highly refined and vary as a function of neurological, physical, and social factors. For the most part, the skills are acquired and in need of development, as opposed to being innate. The types of situations decision makers confront and to which their choices apply range in the amount of cognitive effort, the number and sorts of skills, and typically, the degree of deliberation required to produce desired outcomes.

In light of the fact that the situations decision makers address are so highly variable, to be optimally prepared to function effectively, one needs either to possess, or to acquire, and develop a broad repertoire of pertinent skills. Competence in one skill category may be, and often is, contingent on one's competence in another category. How skillful one is in the management of relationships may, in many instances, depend on how adept he or she is in making sense of situations. The various skills can be discussed separately, within three general categories: task-related, relational, and procedural.

Task-related Skills

Task-related skills concern how individuals and groups manage the substance of the issues with which they grapple. Of the skills that one could classify as task related, four appear to be particularly germane to group decision making: problem recognition and framing, inference-drawing, idea-generation, and argument. Not all of these skills have the same relative importance in every situation involving the need to reach a decision.

If there is an order, it corresponds more directly to the sequence of activities in which groups must engage as decision tasks move from being nearly automatic, routine, or perfunctory to being complex and requiring deliberation than it does to the relative importance of the relevant skills. Against this backdrop, then, is an examination of each of the four task-related skills mentioned earlier.

- ***Problem Recognition And Framing:*** Even if an individual or group's decision-making task reduces merely to determining whether an existing policy, precedent, or standard operating procedure is applicable to a given situation requiring a choice, recognizing what is to be resolved and proper framing of it are important.

Improper recognition or misframing of a problem can have unfortunate consequences.

Decision makers often implement solutions to problems that may or may not exist or that are of an unclear nature. In some instances, decision makers cannot even articulate what it is they are, or were, trying to accomplish by engaging in some action. Problem analysis is one of the greatest deficiencies decision makers commonly display.

Differences in framing can also result in widely discrepant sentencing decisions. These discrepancies suggest that individuals convicted of crimes may, unfortunately either for them or for those they have allegedly victimized, receive penalties that are more or less severe than their acts would merit. Evidence exists to establish that skill in problem recognition and framing is often lacking among decision makers—or, assuming at least that they have such skill, that they do not consistently use it.

When groups engage in decision making, the members often have in mind different framings of the matters to be addressed or issues to be resolved. Decision makers tend to be inconsistent in their application of policies to identical or highly similar problems. They apply policies inconsistently, apparently because they frame the problems they address differently. It is insufficient for decision makers to rely on the possibility that among the different perceptions and, hence, framings of a problem, issue, situation, or the like, one will automatically or necessarily stand out as obviously most accurate.

Proper recognition of what the object of a decision is and how it should be understood requires skill in the interpretation of what signs and signals related to a judgment may indicate. Given that group decision making is interactive, such recognition and understanding require, in addition, that at least one member of the group be able to articulate the problem or issue to be resolved and frame it verbally in a manner that leaves little or no question as to the most reasonable, if not correct, representation.

Framing can determine how conservative or risky individuals or groups are apt to be in making certain kinds of choices and, in the process, act counter to their best interests. Matters framed in terms of losses, for instance, can lead to unduly risky decisions, whereas ones framed in terms of gains often result in excessively conservative choices. Apparently, we are frequently willing to take considerable risks to avoid losses but are reluctant to taken chances if that means foregoing a sure gain, as in the case of one's accepting a firm job offer even when there is a high likelihood that a much better opportunity is in the offing.

Possibly more to the point of the framing–quality of decision relationship, an example can be of an executive who consistently sees a poor profit showing by his company as a production problem when, in fact, it is a sales problem. The misframing leads to an unnecessary investment in improving the product and at the same time a continuation of unacceptable profits. As the example indicates, these sorts of misconstruals can be costly in organizational life. They can be minimized, if not avoided altogether, however, when communication functions to ensure that a group considers the full range of underlying problems that a given set of symptoms may represent and rules out those having the least weight of evidence behind them or smallest degrees of plausibility.

- ***Inference Drawing:*** Although skill in problem-recognition and framing is important to ensure that groups reach appropriate decisions, and in some instances may even be sufficient, the demands of the situation are such that members also have to be skilled in inference drawing. In fact, ability in drawing inferences can be seen as a key to distinguishing between effective and ineffective groups.

Whereas problem recognition and framing reflect one's perceptual and interpretive capabilities, inference drawing extends into the realms of analysis and reasoning and takes the form of descriptive, predictive, analogical, and causal judgments. It is often thought of as equivalent to critical thinking. As the discussion that follows shows, skill in drawing inferences is important not only for the establishment of one's own positions, but also for determining the defensibility of other group members' ideas and the information from which decisions derive.

An inference is a judgment, claim, or conclusion that goes beyond the information on which it is based. Hence, inferences necessarily involve assertions for which validity and truth-value are, at best, somewhat uncertain. An individual or the members of a group making a decision having any degree of consequentiality presumably would want to reduce uncertainty to the extent possible for any inferences on which a choice depends.

There are undoubtedly many reasons for such inferential inadequacies. One that has been especially well researched in recent years, however, is the excessive reliance people place on heuristics in forming judgments. Heuristics are mental shortcuts and rules of thumb that we apply to specific situations requiring judgments.

More important than the specific varieties of the heuristics themselves are the biases that heuristics may induce and the ways those biases can affect decisions. The shortcuts heuristics represent contribute to the emergence of selective information seeking and confirmation bias.

A person who believes that individuals who are accused of crimes are more likely than not to be guilty of them might well be inclined in a trial to focus on evidence indicative of guilt more so than evidence that is exculpatory.

When group members display skill in drawing inferences, they are more likely to make appropriate decisions and to behave rationally. Making appropriate or warranted inferences requires a knowledge of rules of reasoning and an ability to apply them in specific situations. Reasoning by analogy is a form of induction in which a person infers the likelihood that an object or situation will have a particular attribute on the basis of its similarities to other objects or situations that have the attribute.

Such reasoning requires that the similarities outweigh the differences in the objects or situations involved if one is to serve adequately as the basis for drawing some conclusion about the other or others. As another illustration, establishing a cause-to-effect relationship (which may be either inductive or deductive in nature) requires, at minimum, that the alleged cause precede the presumed effect, that the alleged cause and presumed effect be contiguous, and that the alleged cause be sufficient to produce the presumed effect. If one ignores the rules or they do not apply, then his or her inferences are apt to be of questionable validity.

The person must also be able and willing to identify and express what it is that, on logical grounds, make questionable the claims of other group members if, in fact, they are. Knowing the rules for drawing what constitutes a warranted inference and being able to apply them at a cognitive level, as important as such knowledge and skill are, are not sufficient to prevent groups from basing decisions on inferences of questionable merit. The knowledge and related skill must be reflected in the interaction of the group.

In short, one must not only be able but also willing to express the bases on which he or she has arrived at particular judgments concerning such matters as causality and probability, defend the warrants that link evidence to claims, and be open to disconformation under conditions in which others can point to weaknesses in the extent to which relevant information appears to support the judgments to which it leads.

- *Idea Generation:* In addition to possessing and being able to use the task-related skills the prospects for effective decision making in groups are further improved if members, or at least some of them, are adept in generating ideas. This skill can be a valuable asset when it comes to the alternatives groups consider in making choices and establishing the criteria by which they assess those alternatives. Insufficiency in either the number of alternatives or pertinent evaluative criteria can be problematic.

  As an illustration of the importance of ideational skill, consider the case of a family in need of a new car. Were the family to restrict its search, say, to two dealers in an area having 10 or more and to limit its selection criteria also to two (e.g., price and indicated mileage), it would be taking a calculated risk of not making the best possible choice among those realistically available to it. Conceivably, other dealers than the two identified might have lower prices for the same product, the same price, and better mileage for a comparable product or a variety of other combinations that would be to the family's advantage to consider.

  By restricting the criteria, moreover, the family might do something regrettable, such as decide to purchase an automobile that is within its price range and has the mileage desired and then later discover that the service costs are well beyond what they would have been at another dealer and more than offset the price advantage they realised at the time of purchase. Skill in idea generation has been primarily the province of scholars interested in the study of brainstorming.

  Risk taking as a motive for brainstorming (what many refer to as "creative problem solving") gave way to a larger, possibly more critical, concern with increasing the likelihood that the best solutions to problems (or, where appropriate, best alternatives pertaining to issues in need of resolution) would be in the mix. A fundamental premise of brainstorming (and its variants of creative problem solving and idea generation) is that prohibiting the evaluation of ideas at the stage of generation releases creative potential that evaluation typically constricts, or even possibly eliminates.

As a result, for brainstorming to be effective requires the rapid introduction of ideas so as to prevent tendencies toward evaluation to take hold and thereby limit creative thinking. A second premise is that the activity, if individuals seriously undertake it, increases the volume of ideas that members of groups would otherwise identify and consider.

In addition, the proportion of good ideas relative to the total output will be greater than one could expect under more normally constrained processes of ideation. Hence, the probability that a group will have among its alternatives the best possible ones is high, or at least higher than more conventional approaches to problem solving might permit.

Given the potentially inhibiting influence of face-to-face communication, a variation in brainstorming was developed, now commonly referred to as the nominal group technique. In NGT groups, members record ideas in writing and then share them at a later point. This adaptation seems to yield outcomes more nearly in line with the presumption of conventional brainstorming.

Another promising development in the area of idea generation has been the emergence of group support systems (GSS). Although these computer-based, electronic technologies serve a variety of functions in decision-making groups, they seem to be particularly useful as an aid to idea generation. Numerous studies have yielded evidence showing that GSS groups (especially ones using a version called electronic brainstorming) surpass nominal groups and conventional brainstorming groups by a substantial margin in ideational output and quality of ideas. They do so presumably because the technology not only ensures anonymity but also makes it easier for individual members to participate.

Despite the variations in approaches to idea generation and inconsistencies in research findings related to them, decision making groups frequently limit themselves in the alternatives and related ideas they consider, or are even willing to consider, in making choices. Moreover, they do so to a greater degree than is either necessary or desirable. In this regard, the approach to idea generation is far less critical than recognizing the need for members of decision-making groups to expand their thinking and to be active in the search for ideas.

Whatever the conditions under which the members of a decision-making group engage in idea generation, at some point they will need to transform what occurs at a covert, cognitive level into verbal output. If they are unable to translate their thoughts into coherent utterances that reveal their unique qualities and pertinence to the issues under consideration, their introduction will probably be of limited value in, as well as have limited impact on, what subsequently transpires in the decision-making process. As with problem recognition, framing and drawing inferences, then, the successful translation of ideational activity into communicative action is critical to the realization of the potential success of a decision-making group

- ***Argument:*** The skills discussed to this point, if carefully honed, would appear to be sufficient for a group to make appropriate, well-founded, and warranted decisions, presumably by enabling the members to fulfill the requirements typically posed by decision-making tasks. Defining problems, identifying alternatives, quantifying alternatives, applying decision aids, determining what alternative is preferable, and implementing decisions, outlined these requirements as follows:

- Showing correct understanding of the issue to be resolved;
- Determining the minimal characteristics any alternative, to be acceptable, must possess;
- Identifying a relevant and realistic set of alternatives;
- Examining carefully the alternatives in relationship to each previously agreed-upon characteristic of an acceptable choice; and
- Selecting the alternative that analysis reveals to be most likely to have the desired characteristics.

In principle, if a group satisfies the first four requirements, making a decision should be comparatively simple. Ensuring that members have satisfactorily addressed the requirements, however, frequently demands yet another type of skill—that of argument. The necessity of this skill surfaces in a variety of circumstances.

A common situation arising in decision-making groups involves a tendency among members to equate majority positions with correctness, legitimacy, or acceptability. Widespread agreement, moreover, can function to reinforce that belief. A consequence is the exertion of pressure on individuals not sharing the majority view to acquiesce to it. This tendency has been repeatedly documented in the literature on small-group behaviour. Such pressure and resulting acquiescence can be injurious to the prospects for making appropriate decisions if the majority prevails under circumstances in which a dissenting individual, or minority, happens to have the stronger basis in evidence and reasoning for a position other than that of the majority. Dealing effectively with pressure for uniformity therefore can be critical to the success of a decision-making group and requires skill in argument, a skill referred to as "innovative deviance".

Minorities are not inevitably at the mercy of majorities. Skill in argument can contribute to a majority's accepting a minority point of view, that such influence can even carry over into future discussions; and that judgments by members of a minority who are skilled in argument can do much more to raise other arguments and counterarguments than those of the majority. The last of these functions can have the ultimate effect of ensuring that errors have been identified and, if possible, neutralized.

To counteract majority influence, when it is adversely affecting the fulfillment of task requirements, involves more than mere opposition. An individual advancing a minority point of view must also be knowledgeable, confident, consistent, and persistent.

Majorities, when successful, produce compliance, but not necessarily concurrence with, or private acceptance, of their views. Minorities represented by individuals skilled in argument, in contrast, when successful, are more apt to achieve conversion of the majority to the minority positions than when they are represented by individuals who are not skilled in argument.

For argument to play a useful role in decision making, it is not necessary that views of group members be divided along majority and minority lines. Even under conditions in which unanimity exists, it may be important for a group member to enact the role of "devil's advocate". In fact, formalization and routinization of such a role as a safeguard against, and possible deterrent to, the occurrence of groupthink; if not a deterrent, it can function as a measure to reduce groupthink's impact on decisions reached.

Another responsibility of the devil's advocate is to prevent premature consensus, if possible, thereby to aid in keeping groups from taking precipitous and otherwise ill-advised actions.

In line with devil's advocacy, dialectical inquiry has been identified as an argument based approach for overcoming some of the sorts of obstacles to effective decision making noted earlier.

Dialectical inquiry is essentially a process of pitting assumptions underlying decision strategies against counter assumptions and counters strategies that eventuates in an integration of the best surviving ideas. "Dialectical inquiry involves structured debate between the advocates of one plan and the proponents of another plan. The two subgroups debate their different assumptions until they reach agreement." In short, it represents a process that aims at mutual discovery rather than compliance or control of outcomes. For instance, parties to a dispute concerning which of two or more alternatives is to be preferred at initial stages may, in the course of later sustained interaction, begin to see possibilities for combining elements of competing alternatives. In the process, they would have shifted from a distributive (win–lose) to an integrative (win–win) decision-making frame.

Both dialectical inquiry and devil's advocacy move contributory to effective decision making than consensus-based approaches. In both devil's advocacy and dialectical inquiry, argument is central to the process and clearly represents a communicative skill that appears to make a measurable difference in the performance of decision-making groups.

Argument can limit both consensus and commitment to decisions in groups. In light of the demonstrable gains in the quality of decisions in groups in which argument functions, the risks appear to be worth taking. It also appears that when arguments are issue centred and fact based, conversion of the majority, not rejection of the minority, is the more probable result. If these qualities are not evident in the verbalization of arguments, however, their value is likely to be much more limited than if they are. The expression of arguments, in this sense, has to be isomorphic with their underlying characteristics. In other words, if one states an argument in a way that fails to make clear its substantive foundation, the argument is apt to have less impact than if the person states it in a way that does make its substantive foundation clear.

Relational Skills

If all of the obstacles to effective decision making in groups were task related, an individual having skills in the four categories (problem recognition and framing, inference drawing, idea generation and argument) and the ability to transform them into relevant communicative behaviour could have a significant impact on the chances of his or her groups' reaching appropriate or otherwise effective decisions. Lamentably, there are other problems with which one must be prepared to deal. One set of problems tends to be relational in nature. Although representing a different classification, these problems can be every bit as threatening to the interests of fundamentally sound, informed, and constructive decision making as those falling into the task-related category. As a result, they require additional skills, which are designated as leadership, climate building, and conflict management.

- ***Leadership:*** In a sense, every skill identified and discussed so far could be considered an aspect of leadership. Leadership entails not so much engaging in unique activities, but rather doing more of what everyone else in a group does, although not necessarily doing it better.

  The conditions affecting relationship within decision-making groups that arise from the presence of constraints are:

  – *Cognitive constraints* arise when the members of a decision-making group believe themselves to be limited in their capacity to reach decisions because of time, resources, or skill. Under such conditions, the members may develop a collective feeling that results either in hyper vigilance (rush to judgment) or displays of inertia (defensive avoidance). For either response, the relational atmosphere of the group is one characterized by a felt incapacity to succeed in a task and, consequently, a corresponding lack of motivation to perform the task at hand as well as possible.

- *Affiliative constraints* take hold when relationships among group members become a more important concern than successful execution of the task to be performed. Choices may occur in the interest of avoiding hurt feelings or preserving the harmony of the group rather than what the analysis of information relevant to the issues or other matters under consideration suggests.
- *Egocentric constraints* are a result of the surfacing of individuals' needs for control and desire to prevail. Under the influence of egocentric constraints, reaching decisions that, if one is unable to think in favourable terms, have the least unfavourable personal consequences can become more important to members than making good decisions.

When it becomes apparent that one of the aforementioned constraints has taken hold, or is likely to, one should take steps to counteract it. Reducing the impact of relational constraints requires a good deal of interpersonal and communication skill as well as effort. And even if one possesses these qualities, he or she has no assurance of success.

On the other hand, doing nothing can only be detrimental, if not fatal, to the prospects for effective decision making in the long run.

For all three categories of constraints identified, one consequence when they become dominant is that relational concerns, rather than task concerns, drive interaction and do so in ways that increase the probability of poor decisional outcomes.

For instance, if motivation, morale, or the egocentric behaviour of one or more of the members of a decision-making group were to become a focus of attention, the ability of the group as a whole to discharge its task in a propitious manner would be limited.

A group's effective synergy (or the collective energy it can devote to successful task completion) is the difference between its total synergy and the amount it must invest in the members' maintenance needs. A group's actual productivity is the difference between its potential productivity and losses in potential due to process. It should be obvious, then, that task performance suffers in direct proportion to the magnitude of the relational problems the members of a decision-making group encounter—at least theoretically.

A second and related consequence of various constraints' taking hold is that poor or expedient judgments may follow:

- When a group acting in response to a cognitive constraint shows heightened susceptibility to a proposal to let the person in charge make the decision.
- When an affiliative constraint leads group members to do what an individual whose feelings may be hurt wants.
- When an egocentric constraint leads to the view that arguing the merits of case against the position of a person who wants to dominate is not worth the hassle.

A third consequence of cognitive, affiliative, and egocentric constraints is the restriction of interaction. This condition has some invidious implications. Among these are the fact that as participation in decision-making groups becomes increasingly asymmetrical, so, too, does influence. The most talkative members of problem-solving groups usually have the greatest impact on the solutions adopted.

Certain groups perform better when interaction is diffuse rather than restricted. For complex tasks the groups involved function most effectively when the lines of communication among all members are direct and otherwise unrestricted. Hence, it appears that when one or more of the sorts of the constraints has taken hold and is restricting participation, one would be well-advised to try to alter the situation by specifically encouraging both more involvement of all group members and greater focus on task-related concerns.

Such efforts may be more successful if a person acts in a considerate manner. It is also apt to be helpful if one brings some sense of vision to the situation, that is, a verbalization of a desired state in which group members presumably share an interest and that can accrue from making the best possible decision. Finally, one is more likely to achieve positive results if he or she is able to adopt the style of interaction that is best suited to whatever may be inhibiting the efforts of group members to achieve the goal of making a good decision and realizing the vision that led to the goal.

In respect to the last of these points, path–goal theory is helpful in the determination of the style of interaction that is most appropriate to a given situation. From this theoretical perspective, level of motivation is determined by group members' perceptions of their ability to complete a task and the benefits that will derive from doing so. How these sources of motivation combine are indicative of the style of interaction one can most profitably enact. Four such styles have been identified: directive, supportive, participative, and achievement oriented.

To have much chance of being successful in efforts to assure that members of decision-making groups perform effectively, one has to be able to read motivation levels accurately and then select the styles of interaction that are most well-suited to sustaining and, if necessary, restoring movement along a goal path when relational difficulties created by the presence of cognitive, affiliative, and egocentric constraints are inhibiting such movement.

- A *directive style* appears to be most effective when motivation is low due to both perceived limitations in competence and a perceived lack of benefit from performing well.
- A *participative style* seems to be best suited to situations in which the members of a group feel competent and also see personal benefit from successfully completing their tasks.
- A *supportive style* is indicated when group members perceive personal benefit but also see themselves as lacking necessary skills to perform effectively.
- The *achievement-oriented style* appears to have the most favourable consequences when just the opposite conditions pertain, that is, group members see themselves as having the ability to execute a task but no particular benefit to them from doing so.

Leadership Serves Three Functions:

- First, that leadership measurably affects decision making in groups.
- Second, that effective leadership entails the use of skills that enable a person to counteract negative sources of influence stemming from the dominance of cognitive, affiliative, and egocentric constraints.
- Finally, that critical to the successful application of these skills in given situations is one's ability to read relevant cues and to adapt accordingly.

• ***Climate Building:*** In addition to being able to counteract negative sources of influence on the performance of decision-making groups through acts of leadership of the sorts that have been discussed, it is also important that participants promote and be able to contribute to the development of a positive climate. Climate that has been defined as "the prevailing temper, attitudes, and outlook of a dyad, group, or organization" unquestionably affects the quality of performance.

Although decision-making groups functioning in a positive relational climate do not always perform well in the sense of making optimally appropriate choices, the odds that they will are far better than those operating in a negative climate. Ones having low levels of dominance, high task orientation, and friendliness tend to do well. Groups functioning in climates characterized by the opposite conditions do not. The members of decision-making groups, then, take steps to establish positive climates.

Showing sensitivity to and respect for other group members' contributions further aids in the creation and maintenance of a positive climate. When members of decision-making groups feel that they and their input are valued, they show a greater sense of responsibility for and commitment to task completion. One is more likely to develop these feelings when he or she remains relatively unopinionated and also acknowledges the merit in what other group members have to say, even if he or she is in disagreement with them. Moreover, to the extent that one feels obliged to change the views of another, persuasion, rather than coercion, intimidation, and rejection, is the preferable means.

The qualities described here give rise to a spirit of cooperation in decision-making groups, which can, in turn, have a powerful effect on how well they perform.

If individual group members see the social environment in which they are functioning as hostile, they are apt to lose interest in participating. This can be detrimental to the possibilities for effective decision making if those who begin to withhold their participation have knowledge and skills that could aid in the task of making informed choices. Interest and willingness to participate, because of their fragility, can easily decline under normal conditions of interaction; therefore, one should make a conscious effort to avoid engaging in communication that might hasten such decline.

Showing respect for others' ideas and input by the manner in which one discloses his or her reactions to those others' input promotes the development of cohesiveness in groups, commitment to the task, and productivity. So, too, do efforts to legitimate role and status differences when they, of necessity, exist and, when possible, to deemphasize them so as to minimize the probability that individuals having the most power and authority will exert undue influence on decisions reached, which they commonly do. A "we are all in this together" view of a decision-making task can have a strongly salutary effect on performance. Even highly competitive individuals actively promote the development of a positive, supportive climate and show considerable skill in being cooperative if they see groups in which they are members as competitively related to other groups.

Given that displays of respect for others' ideas and input, as well as deemphasizing role and status differences, contribute to the development and maintenance of cohesiveness, one must also be alert to the potential negative effects this quality can have on group performance and take precautions to prevent its becoming excessive. In general, however, cohesiveness is more likely to be an asset than a liability and should be cultivated.

In addition to the value that being sensitive and respectful of others' input has for the development of cohesiveness, commitment, and productivity, such attributes can stimulate and enhance feelings of openness and freedom to participate. When group members feel they are not free to express their views, the quality of decision making may well suffer. One is, therefore, well advised, to engage in communicative acts that encourage willing and thoughtful participation.

Open communication enhances the performance of decision-making and other kinds of groups and hence the quality of the outcomes they achieve.

Although acknowledging that openness and freedom to participate do contribute to more effective performance in task groups, they can also lead to conflict. In that event, if group members are unable to manage the resulting conflicts successfully, then the positive impact of these usually constructive features of a group environment may well be lost. This description here can serve to ameliorate this possibility. Much more important at this point is understanding that climate definitely affects the performance of decision-making groups and that people have a variety of means for contributing to the development of a positive climate. Equally important is that one attempt to cultivate skill in employing these means by how he or she engages others in interaction. Consciously deliberate effort would appear to be a crucial first step.

- ***Conflict Management:*** Even if the climate in which a decision-making group functions is exceptionally positive, from time to time, conflicts of various sorts are almost certain to arise. These conflicts may be intense or comparatively mild. They also may be intellectual, procedural, or interpersonal in nature. Some scholars have reduced the types of conflict that occur in groups to two categories: substantive and affective. A few use the term *cognitive* in place of *substantive*.
  - *Substantive, or cognitive,* conflict derives from differences and other incompatibilities among group members concerning matters related to the agenda. It is typically issue oriented in nature but also frequently encompasses differences and perceived incompatibilities associated with matters of procedure.
  - *Affective, or emotionally based, conflict,* on the other hand, derives from differences and incompatibilities more directly concerned with relationships of group members. Whatever the origin or precise character of a conflict, some sort of management ultimately is required if a group experiencing it is to move forward.

Substantive conflict may appear to be out of place in a discussion of relational skills; however, its successful management frequently, if not always, requires some level of interpersonal adeptness in dealing with the parties involved. Moreover, the principles identified for managing conflict do not, by and large, vary as per the category.

As a result, it seems to be appropriate to include substantive conflict as a condition for which members of a decision-making group may need to exhibit relational skill if they are to resolve successfully problems stemming from its emergence and continued presence.

Conflict, in the context of group decision making, is a state in which there is a fundamental incompatibility in two or more ways of thinking, feeling, or behaving, and members experience pressure to eliminate the incompatibility or otherwise feel some need for uniformity. It is undesirable, perhaps even unacceptable, to permit the incompatibility to remain unaddressed for any length of time if the parties involved are to be able to make a decision at all, let alone a good one.

The mere existence of conflict in decision-making groups is not inherently problematic. In fact, conflict can sometimes be useful in ensuring that task requirements are satisfied or in revealing underlying obstacles in the relationships among group members that are inhibiting progress in the decision-making process.

It is not the presence of conflict, then, about which members of decision-making groups need to be most concerned. Rather, the chief difficulty arises from the failure of group members to move beyond a state of conflict when it is proving to be dysfunctional and is adversely affecting prospects for making well-thought-out and warranted decisions. Whether a conflict is substantive or affective, if left unmanaged, the inattention sooner or later will take its toll on the ability of group members to work collectively toward a common end and may even preclude the possibility for any sort of meaningful action.

Conflict is often a product of diversity and heterogeneity of the parties involved, which is somewhat ironic in light of evidence indicating that heterogeneous groups tend to perform more effectively than homogeneous groups. Be that as it may, when conflict threatens to prevent the members of decision-making groups from completing their tasks or limits their potential to do so, one must be prepared to respond to in a constructive and therefore presumably a pragmatically sound fashion. Unfortunately, members of decision-making groups often avoid dealing with conflicts, apparently in the hope that they will go away, only later to discover that they do not and, in fact, may have become more pronounced.

In addition to avoidance, another common response to conflict in decision-making groups is for the parties involved to adopt a competitive orientation and distributive approach to its management. In short, they see conflicts in terms of winning and losing and as a consequence do what they can to win. Such an approach, however, is not constructive and ill serves the interests of effective decision making.

Approaches that have the potential for inducing cooperation, or at least contribute to an appropriate balance between one's competitive urges and need for cooperation both from and with others, appear to be far superior to ones that do not. Not only do such approaches enable the members of decision-making groups to move beyond a conflict but also subsequently to maintain an atmosphere that is reasonably harmonious and therefore conducive to effective task performance and sound decision-making practices.

Among the approaches that may contribute to the development of a cooperative climate, deliberately avoiding advocacy, avoiding the adoption of win–lose orientations, avoiding capitulation, and avoiding conflict suppres measures such as voting. In addition to these tactics, viewing differences of opinion as positive and easily reached agreement with suspicion can contribute to the development of an environment that promotes better management of conflicts.

Other measures that contribute to the successful management of conflict, communicatively speaking, include:

- Conceiving of conflict and portraying it as an opportunity for problem solving;
- When appropriate, employing palliative strategies, such as indicating that the conflict may not be as severe as the parties to it perceive;
- If possible, shifting the matter at issue from the affective to substantive domain;
- Suggesting more formal negotiation and, if need be, adjudication, of the conflict;
- Showing appropriate concerns for face; and
- Focusing attention on interests rather than positions, that is, considering what competing alternatives have to offer, as opposed to becoming wedded to an initial preference. Far too often, individuals interacting in a conflict situation fail to move past what they want to accomplish to a consideration of what may be in their best interests and, as a consequence, unnecessarily and unfavourably prolong the process. Unfreezing this tendency can make a big difference in how well one ultimately succeeds in managing conflicts that may be interfering with a group's ability to make good decisions.

Implementing these suggestions can help the members of a group manage, if not fully resolve, conflicts by either precluding the emergence of a hostile climate or converting such a climate into one characterized by cooperation and serious effort to overcome the roadblocks that conflicts of various sorts pose. When this sort of condition prevails, better decision making is likely to be the result.

Procedural Skills

Whereas task-related skills reflect the abilities one has to satisfy the substantive requirements of a decision-making task, and relational skills pertain to the management of interpersonal difficulties posed by the members of groups, procedural skills concern how the members go about performing the task. In short, procedural skills are ones that come into play in those instances in which groups have to undertake actions in some sensible sequence to progress from a starting point (typically a discussion question or issue) to a destination (decision or choice). How well they succeed often depends on the sensitivity members display in recognizing what is necessary to progress along their goal path and in selecting communicative interventions that have the effect of sustaining such movement.

Although procedural skills—or at least some aspects of them—are not ordinarily thought of in communicative terms, abilities representing this category, as in the case of some of those included under the headings of task-related and relational skills, surface and become evident in one's interactions with others. For instance, even planning, which some individuals might not regard as having any communicative significance, is an activity considered to be an aspect of decision making that often does, and properly should, take place in discussion.

Process enactment, a second feature of group decision making requiring procedural skills, entails efforts to determine whether the mechanisms in place for moving a group forward are, in fact, contributing to the furtherance of a decision-making task and, if not, making the necessary adaptations to ensure that they do. Hence, communication is clearly and necessarily implicated in one's demonstration of this category of procedural skill.

Planning

Planning in the context of decision making is the process by which one or more members of a group determine how to complete its task and what otherwise to achieve a desired goal. Specifically, planning entails a set of actions with the aim of identifying and ordering the means by which a group will attempt to move from an issue to be resolved to a conclusion concerning its resolution, as well as creating the conditions that are necessary for such movement. In this sense, planning is itself a form of decision making (more properly meta–decision making) concerning how to make other kinds of decisions.

Large numbers of groups do not take planning seriously. This kind of disregard for planning is unfortunate. Even a limited amount of planning can improve group performance significantly. Planning has a substantial measurable impact on group performance.

These included efficiency, coordination of effort, retention of a task focus, and level of organizational development. The conditions under which planning occurs appear to represent an aspect of the process to which one needs to be attuned and prepared to monitor. The use of technological innovations, such as computer-mediated communication and group decision support systems, improves group performance. Planning particularly in regard to procedures should taken serously. The procedure a group adopts can have significant consequences for the quality of decision it reaches. Therefore, groups that pay attention to how they are going to perform decision-making tasks may better their chances for being effective.

The act of planning, in and of itself, is not the source of increased effectiveness of decision-making groups. Rather, it is the quality of planning, as well as the capability planners exhibit, both in the selection of procedures to follow and in communicating to others that following them is worthwhile in respect to the outcomes, that makes the difference. Several considerations pertinent to the question of quality and what may enhance it in the context of planning for decision-making discussions follow.

As part of the planning process, one needs to be clear in identifying goals and stating objectives, because, the particular ways in which groups articulate goals and objectives can influence other aspects of the decision-making process, e.g., selection of the criteria and identification of alternatives group members consider. One should also make an effort in advance of discussion to achieve concurrence with the goals and objectives as stated, but be willing to modify them in the face of nonconcurrence. In this way, the planner avoids initial confusion and limits the prospects for later conflicts.

In making plans for group decision making, a person needs to be sensitive to what approaches and rules are best suited for the specific task the group is to perform. For instance, one needs to be aware of whether unanimity, as opposed to majority rule, is appropriate for a given task. Majority rule enables groups to take action, but there is no assurance that the majority will have fulfilled task requirements in the manner effective decision making presumes. Instead, majority rule could simply enable those with superior numbers to impose a decision. Hence, what in certain respects is an asset could also prove to be a liability.

Consensus, in some instances, may make it more difficult for a group to reach a decision, but the rule may also increase the likelihood that the group will have given careful thought to task requirements. On the other hand, requiring consensus may only serve to prolong discussion and eventually lead to a decision that represents not the best possible choice, but instead the lowest common denominator, that is, the only alternative all members are willing to endorse. In deciding by consensus, group members also have to be careful not to fall victim to the "consensus-implies-correctness heuristic". An individual skilled in planning will be alert to such possibilities and convey as adroitly as possible the associated risks to other members of a decision-making group.

As another example, were a decision-making group to be in need of a good deal of idea-generation for identifying criteria and alternatives, an important aspect of the planning process would be the form to be followed.

There is a need to recognize the limitations in procedures available to decision makers, to use that awareness in the planning process, and to communicate clearly how those limitations have influenced choices concerning which procedures to employ and which not to employ. Failure to do so can result in poor planning and serve to reinforce the already too prevalent feeling that planning is a waste of time.

Process Enactment

As important as planning is, perhaps the strongest evidence of procedural skill arises in the enactment of the process of group decision making. However well motivated the members of a group may be to operate within agreed-on plans and approaches to performing their task, decision-making discussions seldom go completely according to plan. Often, they deviate substantially. In part, this occurs because of unforeseen developments that arise in the course of performing a task. It can also occur, because individuals experience difficulty in enacting plans in the abstract. This condition, however, does not preclude the possibilities for a group's moving forward in an efficient and effective manner; rather, it requires a different level of procedural skill. Under such circumstances, members who are high in procedural sensitivity, as well as who take steps to address process disruptions resulting from procedural problems, can prove to be invaluable.

Although some scholars have posited a direct relationship between the quality of procedures decision-making groups employ and the quality of their decisions, people vary in the significance they attach to procedural concerns. One should not, however, draw the conclusion that any order in which the members of a group perform a decision-making task is conducive to reaching a desirable outcome or that one need not be concerned about how such a group goes about performing its task. It is important to develop skill in being able to restore a decision-making group's movement along a goal-path known to improve the odds for achieving desired outcomes when the members have deviated from that path.

The exact order in which group members address requirements is less critical than efforts to make certain that the requirements receive attention. Procedures have a connection to, as well as bearing on, how well the members of decision-making groups perform. Vigilance represents the attention decision makers display to the requirements of their task. The more vigilant they are, the fewer the symptoms of defective decision making they are apt to exhibit, and the more likely they are to make good decisions. The skill necessary to have measurable impact in redirecting a group's activities in productive directions, does not require an extraordinary level of development; rather, it is within fairly easy reach of anyone who has a reasonable understanding of the requirements a decision-making group must fulfill to be effective.

Procedure clearly seems to matter, and individuals who take steps to see that the process by which groups attempt to arrive at decisions is enacted appropriately and in accordance with practices based on acknowledged principles of sound decision making play a critical role. At the very least, they help to minimize the prospects that inappropriate decisions will be the product of behaviour that, in most instances, should be reasonably easy to alter once those involved become aware of it.

Conclusion

Being an effective contributor to group decision-making discussions requires a variety of skills that one exhibits by means of his or her communicative behaviour. Such skills are grouped in three categories: task-related, relational, and procedural.

Among the skills that fit the category "task-related" are problem-recognition and framing, inference-drawing, idea-generation, and argument. Participants in decisionmaking discussions who (*a*) accurately understand and articulate what the task requires of their group, (*b*) draw and clearly express the conclusions that proper analysis of relevant information warrants, (*c*) think creatively and imaginatively in identifying possible means for resolving issues under consideration, and (*d*) convincingly present and advance positions related to the issues contribute substantially more to the group's effectiveness than those lacking such skill or who fail to exhibit them.

The relational skills that have been addressed are leadership, climate-building, and conflict management. Individuals skilled in leadership use communication to counteract negative sources of influence stemming from constraints posed by the task, relationships among group members, and the motivations of particular individuals. In addition to needing members who able to counteract the sorts of negative influences, decision-making groups' chances for performing effectively increase when one or more of the participants communicates in ways that enhance the climate of interaction. A positive climate is one in which interaction exhibits such qualities as friendliness, mutual respect, low levels of dominance, openness to ideas, and willingness to cooperate. Finally, the interests of effective decision making are advanced when group members, via their communicative behaviour, are able to:

- Confront rather than avoid conflict,
- Engage in it at a substantive level,
- Recognize the situations in which it may function constructively, and
- Adopt integrative, as opposed to distributive, approaches in attempting to manage it.

As important as task-related and relational skills are to the success of decisionmaking groups, unless they are accompanied by well-developed procedural skills, such groups can still perform poorly. Procedural skills exist at two levels: planning and process enactment. Planning entails not only such routine activities as setting goals, forming an agenda, selecting the procedures to be followed, scheduling, arranging for necessary equipment or materials, and ensuring a comfortable physical environment, but also giving thought to probable occurrences in discussion and how to deal with them, should they arise. No matter how careful the planning for a decision-making discussion is, the performance of a task can go awry. Averting that possibility requires that participants be able to deal with procedural problems as they arise. Providing orientation or direction, noting situations in which task requirements are receiving inadequate attention, enacting the role of "reminder" when participants lose sight of the procedures they have agreed to follow, and generally maintaining a high level of vigilance throughout a decision-making are all indicative of an individual who is skilled in process enactment.

Having members who possess and use the skills identified earlier provides no guarantee that a decision-making group will make the best possible choices in its deliberations. The material covered, however, makes clear that the exhibition of such skills substantially improves prospects for a group's doing so. It also make clear that the absence of these skills restricts communication to being little more a medium of exchange. In contrast, having and employing the sorts of skills noted contributes to its being a valuable instrument of informed choice.

Interaction in groups is more likely to result in good decisions when members possess and are able to use such skills than when they either do not possess them or fail to use the ones they have to good advantage. Cultivation of the skills considered comes with experience and opportunity to take part in group decision making. What seems to be more important at an initial stage, however, is the knowledge of what those skills are and how they relate to the outcomes members of decision-making groups achieve. Groups are capable of extraordinary accomplishment, but such accomplishment depends heavily on the capabilities of the members.

GROUP DISCUSSION

How To Speak Properly During Group Discussions

Speech plays an important role in our ability to communicate as humans. This is especially important when we get together in groups. During group discussions, the speech you use can have a powerful impact on the way your message is received by those who listen to you.

The cultural background of an individual will also play a role in how they speak. When group discussion are held, there are a number of things you will want to remember about your speech. First, it is important to make sure you speak clearly. Those who listen to you will need to understand what you are saying.

Because most group discussions are restricted to time, it will become tedious to both you and the other members if you have to repeat what you are saying because they do not understand you. This could be a major problem for someone who is speaking a language that is not their native tongue. When you make a statement, it is important to make sure you speak clearly. It is also important to be concise. Speak in a manner that will allow the other members to understand exactly what you are saying.

This should occur the first time you make a statement. You should not have to repeat yourself.

It is also important to speak audibly. Everyone should be able to hear what you are saying. If somone has to ask you to speak up, you will be forced to repeat yourself, and this will waste time. If someone makes a statement that you do not understand, ask them to clarify in a polite manner. During group discussions, it isn't just enough to speak eloquently. It is also important to make sure you speak in a proper tone. If you speak in a harsh manner, you can send across the wrong message to others who are participating in the discussion. This could lead to conflicts, and it is important to avoid this. The tone of your voice and the way you speak will say a lot about how you feel about a certain topic, and it will also show how well you can speak.

If you don't speak in an intelligent manner, the other members may assume that you are unintelligent, even if that is not the case. If you need to interrupt someone who is speaking, it is always important to interject their conversation in a nice way. Some groups may require you to raise your hand and be called upon before you can comment on a statement or idea. If you disagree with a statement that has been made, do it in a manner that is tactful. Always talk in a manner that is courteous to others. You should not ridicule or attack someone personally because you don't like their idea.

If you are the head of the discussion group, it is very crucial for you to speak properly. Even though the group should be responsible for making the final decision, the members will look to you to lead them. If you cannot speak in a proper manner, your leadership abilities may be questioned. If you have to repeat yourself to the group, this will delay the amount of time it takes for the group to achieve important goals. If you are speaking about a topic that is complex, it may be helpful to use analogies that can help the members grasp the concept.

While it is important to speak eloquently, you will want to avoid using technical terms that are not understood by the group. Being able to explain complicated concepts in a simple manner will allow the group to quickly grasp what you are trying to tell them.

Group Decision–Making And Collective Induction

Consider small groups of scientific researchers, weather forecasters, petroleum geologists, securities analysts, political prognosticators, market researchers, auditors, intelligence analysts, corporate board members, or air crash investigators. Although the objectives and task domains of these groups vary greatly, all of them engage in *collective induction*, the cooperative search for descriptive, predictive, and explanatory generalizations, rules, and principles. In the process of *induction*, all of these groups observe patterns, regularities, and relationships in some domain, propose hypotheses to account for them, and evaluate the hypotheses by observation or experiment. In the process of *collective* induction, all of these groups map a distribution of group member hypotheses into a single group response by some social combination process.

A Theory of Group Decision–Making

- ***Postulate 1:*** Cooperative decision-making groups may resolve disagreement among their members in formulating a collective group response in five ways:
  - Random selection among proposed alternatives,
  - Voting among proposed alternatives,
  - Turn taking among proposed alternatives,
  - Demonstration of preferability of a proposed alternative, and
  - Generation of a new emergent alternative.

  The essential process in all group decision making, large or small, formal or informal, important or trivial, cooperative, mixed-motive, or competitive, is the resolution of disagreement among the group members. Postulate 1 proposes that there are five essential ways by which freely interacting cooperative groups whose members have equal formal status and power may resolve this disagreement. Generation of a new emergent alternative includes a wide variety of processes such as averaging, compromising, or logrolling. Postulate 1 concerns only cooperative decision making, rather than mixed-motive and competitive decision making, for which possible modes of resolution of disagreement include coercion, bribery, combat by representative champions, excommunication, and warfare. With these qualifications, Postulate 1 proposes that these five ways of resolution of disagreement are exhaustive. Following the current general term for theory and research on small-group performance and processes, Postulate 1 concerns group decision making, although the same area was previously called group problem solving, as in the comprehensive review of Kelley and Thibaut.

- ***Postulate** 2*: The five ways of resolving disagreement may be formalized by social combination models:
  - Random selection: equiprobability model,
  - Voting: majority and plurality models,
  - Turn taking: proportionality model,
  - Demonstration: truth wins and truth-supported wins models, and
  - Generation of a new emergent alternative: specified probability of an alternative not proposed by any member.

  Postulate 2: Elaborates the fundamental assumption of a social combination approach to group decision making, that group processes may be considered as a social combination process that maps a distribution of group member preferences onto a single collective group response.
- ***Postulate 3:*** Cooperative group tasks may be ordered on a continuum anchored by intellective and judgmental tasks.

  Intellective tasks are problems or decisions for which there exists a demonstrably correct solution within a verbal or quantitative conceptual system.

  Intellective tasks emphasize the solution of a problem by a series of permissible operations within some set of constraints. Problem solution is defined by the relationships of the conceptual system within which the problem is embedded. The objective for the group is to achieve the correct solution, and the criterion of group success is whether or not the solution is achieved.

Judgmental tasks are evaluative, behavioural, or aesthetic judgments for which a demonstrably correct response does not exist. Examples include virtually all of the tasks in research on decision under uncertainty, the choice shift and group polarization, mock jury decisions, and attitudes. On judgmental tasks the objective for the group is to achieve consensus, and the criterion of group success is whether or not consensus is achieved. For example, a jury that fails to reach consensus ("hangs") has failed to achieve the objective of a jury trial.

In summary, Postulate 3 proposes that intellective and judgmental tasks are the endpoints of a continuum rather than a dichotomy.

- ***Postulate 4:*** A demonstrably correct response requires four conditions:
  - Group consensus on a conceptual system,
  - Sufficient information,
  - That incorrect members are able to recognize the correct response if it is proposed, and
  - That correct members have sufficient ability, motivation, and time to demonstrate the correct response to the incorrect members.

Demonstrability presupposes previous group consensus on a conceptual system. A verbal conceptual system such as a language or constitution assumes consensus on the vocabulary, syntax, and relationships of the system. A mathematical system such as a geometry or algebra assumes consensus on the primitive terms, axioms, and operations of the system.

Given this consensus on the system, there must be sufficient information for solution. A system of two simultaneous equations in two unknowns has a unique solution, but one equation in two unknowns does not. The group members who do not know the correct response must have sufficient understanding of the system to recognize and accept a correct answer if it is proposed by another member. Finally, Postulate 4 specifies the characteristics of the group members that are necessary for them to demonstrate the correct response to the incorrect members.

- ***Postulate 5***: The number of group members that is necessary and sufficient for a collective decision is inversely proportional to the demonstrability of the proposed group response.

  Two-thirds majority, in which the group decision is that favoured by two thirds of the group members, is the best-fitting social combination process for jury decisions. Juries without a two-thirds majority typically either are unable to come to a decision ("hang") or give the defendant the benefit of the doubt and acquit. Jury decisions are judgmental tasks because conviction or acquittal is typically a matter of the more credible and persuasive rival scenario rather than a demonstrably correct response.

  Simple majority, in which the group decision is that favoured by more than half of the group members, is the best-fitting social combination process for attitudinal judgments and preferences among bets, especially when the majority position is in the direction of prevailing values or norms. Attitudinal judgments and preferences among bets are judgmental tasks because they are based on values rather than demonstrably correct answers.

  Most of this research with jury decisions, attitudinal judgments, and preferences among bets has involved two response alternatives, such as conviction or acquittal. An important exception is the four verdict categories (first-degree murder, second-degree murder, manslaughter, not guilty by reason of self-defence). Although a majority social combination process fit very well for decisions of guilty (collapsing over the first three verdict categories) versus not guilty, a plurality process fit quite well when there was no majority for one of the four verdicts. This suggests a simple majority, plurality otherwise, social combination process for tasks with nondemonstrable answers and more than two response categories.

Truth-supported wins, in which two correct numbers are necessary and sufficient for a correct group response, is the best-fitting social combination process on general world knowledge, vocabulary, and analogy items.

These tasks fit the four conditions of demonstrability of Postulate 4, but the correct answers are not intuitively obvious or immediately evident once proposed, so a correct member must be supported by another member to persuade the incorrect members to adopt the correct answer as the group response.

Truth wins, in which one correct member is necessary and sufficient for a correct group response, is the best-fitting social combination process on insight or "Eureka" puzzles, creativity tasks, and mathematical problems. These tasks fit first two conditions of Postulate 4, and have correct answers that are either intuitively and immediately obvious to the incorrect members (third condition) or demonstrable by a single correct member (fourth condition).

Fewer group members are necessary for a group solution when they believe that a correct answer exists in solving a murder mystery (intellective task) than when they believe that a correct answer does not exist and they are gathering evidence for a possible indictment by a grand jury (judgmental task).

More generally, we may conjecture that the well-established finding that groups predominantly discuss shared information supporting a less optimal decision rather than discuss and integrate distributed information supporting a more optimal decision may apply relatively more to tasks near the judgmental end of the continuum of Postulate 3 than to tasks near the intellective end.

In summary, a wide range of group tasks supports the generalization of Postulate 5 that the number of group members that is necessary and sufficient for a group response is inversely proportional to the demonstrability of the response. The conditions of demonstrability are specified by Postulate 4. Tasks at the intellective end of the continuum of Postulate 3 require the fewest members for a (correct) group response, and tasks at the judgmental end of the continuum require the most members for a (consensual) group response. Within the context of this general social combination theory of group decision making we now specifically consider collective induction.

□□

Chapter 13

Making Communication Effective

CREATIVITY IN COMMUNICATION: A THEORETICAL FRAMEWORK FOR COLLABORATIVE PRODUCT CREATION

Most creative acts occur in a collaborative context. Recent research contributions the relevance of collaborative creativity but they lack a theoretical basis. What exactly is understood by collaborative creativity and above all, how it is examined, appears not to be the focus of well-founded analyses. The key objective here is to present a new model characterizing collaborative product creation. This model describes theoretical essence needed for any creative collaboration. As a result, the phenomenon of communication is crystallized as the driving force for collaborative creativity.

CREATIVE COMMUNICATION SKILLS

Creative Communication Skills Objectives Include:

- Raise Awareness
- Understand Communication Dynamics
- Work with Body Language
- Deal with Assumptions
- Work with Differing Points of View
- Understand Patterns, Habits and Beliefs
- Develop Great Listening and Responding Skills

- Develop Individual Strengths and Qualities
- Understand Active vs. Passive Choosing
- Use Positive Reinforcement
- Manage Conflict
- Being More In Charge
- Gain Confidence

Companies talk about needing better communication skills, but often don't know exactly what that means or they don't know how to go about making it happen. And without doubt, unless you are a company of one, at some point or another, communication will go awry through no one's fault or intention - it's just the way it happens. If you have groups of people who simply have to communicate more effectively then giving them communication training may be just what you need.

Communication is probably not something you would instantly equate with creativity. It's something that we do throughout our lives, but often don't give much thought to how we're doing it. But communication is a skill (and perhaps an art), and like any other skill, we can improve upon it.

With better communication, we can enhance our relationships, both personal and business. And since just about everything in life is based on relationship, the impact of improved communication can be far-reaching.

One of the primary factors in good communication is listening. Listening is hearing, but with the added component of seeking to understand what the other person is communicating. We achieve this by listening with the intent to understand, rather than thinking about our reaction or response to the communication. The result is that the other person feels that we are interested in them and what they have to say. By paying attention, we can pick up clues about the person and what they are saying that will forward the conversation and help create relationship.

It's also important to note that communication is a two-way street. Speaking is only half the picture; the message needs to be acknowledged in order to be complete. When someone else is speaking, you can let them know you're receiving their communication by focusing your attention on them and perhaps adding an occasional nod or saying "uh-huh" to let them know you're with them (this is particularly important on the phone, where the speaker is otherwise met by dead silence).

Part of becoming conscious of good communication is being aware of the barriers. Several categories to consider are:

- ***Environmental***: There are times when the environment is not conducive to certain kinds of communication. For example, a noisy restaurant is not the place for an intimate, meaningful conversation. Likewise, the office may not be the best place to discuss personal issues.
- ***Preoccupation With One's Own Thoughts:*** Often as we listen to someone, our minds is busy planning how we will respond. Or we're off thinking about a personal issue that's on our mind or in a past memory that the conversation has triggered. When we do that, we're not fully present and miss a lot of what is said. This is an example of hearing rather than listening.
- ***Personal Judgments And Biases***: As with preoccupation, as someone is speaking, we may find ourselves off in our head, having a running monologue judging what the person is saying. "I like that", I don't like that, "I don't agree" and harsher judgments fill our mind. Or we may have personal biases about what the person is saying, or about the person him or herself, that block us from really listening to what is being said.
- ***Cultural Factors***: Different cultures have different styles of communication, including use of words and body language. We may misinterpret what is said or even take offense. The person's gestures, or lack of them, may be distracting. The language barrier itself or a difficult-to-understand accent may also cause us to "tune out" and lose what's being said.
- ***Low self-esteem:*** If you feel unworthy, and therefore intimidated by the person you're speaking with, it's hard for the communication to flow. Your attention tends to

be on yourself — what you're saying, how you look, what they think of you — and not on really listening to what's being said.

PRESENTATION SKILLS

There are six clusters which form the main elements of good, effective presentation skills.

Profile The Occasion, Audience And Location

You should ask yourself these questions:

- *The Occasion*
  - — What kind is it?
  - — What are the aims of it?
  - — What time is allowed?
  - — What else is happening?
- *The Audience*
  - — Do they know anything about you?
  - — Do you know its size?
  - — What do they expect?
  - — Why are they there?
  - — What is their knowledge level?
  - — Do you know any one personally/professionally?
  - — Do you expect friendliness, indifference or hostility?
  - — Will they be able to use what they hear?
- *The location*
  - — Do you know the room size, seating arrangement, lay-out/set-up and acoustics?
  - — Do you know the technical arrangements for use of microphones, audio-visuals, lighting and whether assistance is available (and have you notified in advance your requirements)?
  - — Do you know who will control room temperature, lighting and moving people in and out?
  - — Have you seen/should you see it?

Plan And Write The Presentation

Elements to address are:

- ***Deciding Your Objective Which Needs To Be***
  - Clear
  - Specific
  - Measurable
  - Achievable in the time available
  - Realistic
  - Challenging
  - Worthwhile
  - Participative
- ***Making A Plan With A Framework Which Has***
  - A beginning (including introductory remarks, statement of objectives and relevance and an outline of the presentation(s)).
  - A middle (divided into up to six sections maximum, ensuring main points are illustrated and supported by examples or evidence, use summaries and consider time allocation carefully — and test it).
  - An end (summarize, linking conclusions with objectives and end on a high note).

Use Visual Aids

As up to 50 per cent of information is taken in through the eyes, careful consideration should be given to the clear, simple and vivid use of audio-visuals. Useful tips are:

- Overhead/projector/computer slides help make a point and keep eye contact with an audience (look at the people not the slides).
- Only present essential information in this way (keep content to about 25 words or equivalent if in figures).
- Have them prepared with appropriate professionalism.
- Know the order.

- Use pictures and colour if possible.
- Do not leave a visual aid on for too long.

Some difficulties with the different types of audio-visual equipment are:

- ***Overhead Projection***: Ease of use and flexibility can be offset by poor quality images and problems in using well.
- ***Computer Generated or 35mm Slide Projection:*** Professional in appearance, good for large audiences and ease of use with a remote control can be offset by the need for dim lights (making note-taking difficult) and lack of flexibility in changing the order of viewing.
- ***Flipcharts***: Easy to use and informal but difficult to use successfully with large groups, and generally do not look professional and take up time to use.
- ***Tape Decks/Videos***: Can provide variety but difficult to set-up and synchronise, especially without technical support.

Prepare Your Talk

In preparing your talk you need to decide whether you are to present with a full script, notes or from memory. This depends on the occasion and purpose of the presentation but whichever method is chosen, it is always acceptable to refer to your fuller notes if needs be during a presentation.

Notes on cards or on slide/flipcharts can be used as memory joggers if you present without notes. If you are required to read a paper, at least be able to look up occasionally. Remember that failing to prepare is preparing to fail.

Rehearse With Others

Rehearsal is important, but not so much that spontaneity is killed and naturalness suffers, to ensure the presentation (and any audio-visual aid) is actually going to work in practice. You should always visit the location if at all possible and check that everything works — knowing the location is as important as rehearsing the presentation, indeed it is an essential part of the rehearsal.

Delivery On The Day

If you find you are nervous (and this is normal), experiencing fear and its physical manifestations, remember to:

- Breathe deeply
- Manage your hands
- Look at your audience
- Move well
- Talk slowly
- Compose and relax yourself
- Remember that the audience is invariably on your side
- Project forward to the end of the presentation and picture the audience applauding at the end.

Overall you should ensure that your presentations contain:

- *Beginning*: Introduces yourself properly, captures the audience and gives the background, objectives and outline of your talk.
- *Middle*: Is kept moving along (indicating whether questions are to be asked as-you-go or at the end) with eye contact over the whole audience, at a reasonable pace, with a varying voice and obvious enjoyment on your part.
- *End*: Is signaled clearly then goes off with a memorized flourish.
- *Questions*: Are audible to all (or repeated if not), answered with conciseness, stimulated by yourself asking some questions, dealt with courteously and with the lights on.
- *Conclusion*: Is a strong summary of talk and questions/ discussions and closes with words of thanks.

STRENGTHENING MOTIVATION THROUGH COMMUNICATION

The mere possession of communication media, however, will do little to accomplish the objective of good communication. You may have all the communication tools needed to communicate information and ideas with great proficiency, but the fact remains, nevertheless, that they are not affecting attitudes and behaviour as they should. Obviously, the answer to today's communication problems lies not in the media we possess, but in how we use these media.

□□

Chapter 14

Understanding Gestures

You need to know more about the cross-cultural communication process, and consider body language, gestures, and active listening. Considering that communication is something you do every day, how many people actually stop to consider what is happening before they speak? Can you just talk without thinking too much about the target audience, the message to be communicated, and a host of other information? Communication is too important to be left to chance. The subtleties of language, expressions, and gestures all enrich the content of what you are saying. Of course, when you're communicating on a global scale, you need to be sure that what you're saying—and the way you say it—will not cause offense to your cross-cultural audience.

CONSTRUCTING COMMUNICATION BY GESTURES

People move their hands as they talk – they gesture. Gesturing is a robust phenomenon, found across cultures, ages, and tasks. Gesture is even found in individuals blind from birth. But what purpose, if any, does gesture serve? Gesture on its own, substitute for speech and clearly serve a communicative function. When called upon to carry the full burden of communication, gesture assumes a language-like form, with structure at word and sentence levels. However, when produced along with speech, gesture assumes a different form – it becomes imagistic and analog. Despite its form, the gesture that accompanies speech also communicates. Trained coders can glean substantive information from gesture – information that is not always identical to that gleaned from speech. Gesture can thus serve as a research tool, shedding light on speakers' unspoken thoughts. The controversial question is whether gesture conveys information to listeners *not* trained to read them. Do spontaneous gestures communicate to ordinary listeners? Or might they be produced only for speakers themselves? I suggest these are not mutually exclusive functions – gesture serves as both a tool for communication for listeners, and a tool for thinking for speakers.

The language model of the community exerts less influence on the child. The gesture systems constructed by deaf children who are unable to acquire speech and have not been exposed to a sign language can be explained. These children are constructing their communication systems in large part without benefit of conventional linguistic input. As a result, the children's gestures reflect skills that they themselves bring to the language-learning situation, skills that interact with linguistic input when that input is available. The gestures that hearing children produce when they talk can also be explained. Gesture does not need to assume a language-like role for these children and indeed it does not. Nevertheless, the gestures these speaking children produce convey information and that information is often different from the information found in their talk. Gesture thus allows the children to reach beyond the confines of the language they are speaking. Both cases highlight the child's contribution to the communication process and provide unique opportunities to observe the child's skills as language-maker.

USING BODY LANGUAGE

Some research estimates that as much as 93 percent of your message's impact depends on non–verbal elements. This includes facial expressions, body movement, vocal cues, and proxemics.

Body language and gestures are an innate part of our psyche. There have been many interesting studies conducted on body language and the use of gestures. In one particular experiment, twelve children with perfect vision and twelve children who were blind since birth were observed to see whether either group gestured more than the other. The results showed that the blind children actually gestured just as much as their full-sighted counterparts, even when they knowingly spoke with other blind children. The researchers concluded that gesturing is an innate part of our expressive and communicative patterns, and that speech and body language are highly interconnected.

There is a direct correlation between our ability to read body language and our relationships. In another study, college students were tested to see whether they could accurately identify the meanings behind certain facial expressions and tones of voice. Significantly, the research consistently showed that the students who made the most errors in interpreting the meanings were those who had troubled relationships and/or greater feelings of depression.

Eyes

Ralph Waldo Emerson said, "The eyes of men converse as much as their tongues." The more common phrase we hear is the "eyes are the windows to the soul". Through our eyes, we can gauge the truthfulness, intelligence, attitude, and feelings of a speaker. Not making eye contact when we ought to can have devastating results. Note the following true example:

Our eyes' pupils are one of the most sensitive and complicated parts of our body. They react to light but they also respond to our emotions, betraying a variety of feelings. When a person is aroused, interested, and receptive, the pupils dilate. This is an attempt by the eye to allow the entry of more light and more information. Being able to see each other's pupils is so important to our communication that we often distrust a person wearing sunglasses. Consciously or subconsciously, we assume that use of the glasses is a direct attempt to hide the eyes in fear that they will reveal the truth.

Making eye contact can also convey love or passion. In a number of studies on eye contact and attraction, researchers found that simply looking into one another's eyes can create passionate feelings. In one particular case, two members of the opposite sex who were complete strangers were found to have amorous feelings toward each other after merely gazing into one another's eyes. In another study, beggars were interviewed about their "tactics" for getting donations from passersby. Several of the beggars stated that one of the very first things they tried to do was establish eye contact. They claimed that making eye contact made it harder for people to pretend they hadn't seen them, to ignore them, or to just keep walking. Other studies have shown that public speakers who make more eye contact, use pleasant facial expressions, and incorporate appropriate gestures into their speeches have more persuasive power than speakers who do not.

Hands

The way we use our hands tells others a lot about what we are thinking or feeling. If your hands are tucked away in your pockets or behind your back, you may be perceived as holding something back. Clenched fists may portray anger or tension. Holding your hands up around your face—over your mouth, by your ear, etc.—may portray dishonesty. Stroking your chin shows you are thinking about what has been said. If you place your hands flat on the table in front of you, you may be sending a signal that you agree. On the other hand, placing your hands on your hips may express defiance or dominance.

Head

If you notice your prospect tilting her head toward you, it is very likely that she is interested in the deal. If her head is tilted away, however, she may not be totally sold, and, in fact, she may feel some distrust or dissatisfaction toward you or the offer. If she rests her head on her hand, she is bored or not really interested. If she keeps looking around, you can bet she is most likely thinking: "Get me out of here". Obviously, nodding her head would express agreement and interest.

Legs

If your prospect is pointing his feet in your direction, he is most likely facing you and is therefore likely to be very interested in your offer. If his legs or feet are pointed away from you, however, he may just be enduring your pitch and may be feeling ready to leave as soon as he has the opportunity. If his legs are crossed when he stands, he may still be feeling some awkwardness about the deal. On the other hand, if his legs are crossed when he is seated, he may be feeling some resistance to you or your offer. If he keeps tapping his foot, he's either wishing you would shut up and let him talk or he's feeling bored.

Consider the Following

- Leaning closer = interest and comfort
- Learning away = discomfort with the facts or with the person presenting them
- Nodding = interest, agreement, and understanding
- Relaxed posture = openness to communicate
- Hand to cheek = evaluating or considering
- Sitting with hands clasped behind head = arrogance or superiority
- Tapping or drumming fingers = impatience or annoyance
- Steepling fingers = closing off or creating barrier
- Fidgeting = boredom, nervousness, or impatience
- Clutching objects tightly = anxiety or nervous anticipation
- Chin stroke = deep thinking or intently listening

From what we have discussed, you can see that resistance can be easily detected in your prospect. Check to see if your prospect's body is leaning away from you. Observe whether she faces you at an angle. Look to see whether her arms, legs, or both are crossed. She may glance from the corner of the eye and make minimal eye contact. She may tap her finger or foot—or her feet may point away from you. Generally, if she is resisting your persuasive efforts, her posture is closed. When you persuade, avoid adopting this body language.

Learning how to persuade and influence will make the

difference between hoping for a better income and having a better income. Beware of the common mistakes presenters and persuaders commit that cause them to lose the deal.

CONCLUSION

Persuasion is the missing puzzle piece that will crack the code to dramatically increase your income, improve your relationships, and help you get what you want, when you want, and win friends for life. Ask yourself how much money and income you have lost because of your inability to persuade and influence. Think about it. Sure you've seen some success, but think of the times you couldn't get it done. Has there ever been a time when you did not get your point across? Were you unable to convince someone to do something? Have you reached your full potential? Are you able to motivate yourself and others to achieve more and accomplish their goals? What about your relationships? Imagine being able to overcome objections before they happen, know what your prospect is thinking and feeling, feel more confident in your ability to persuade.

BENEFITS OF UNDERSTANDING GESTURES

Communication is an integral part of your life, affecting everything about what you think, say, and do; and body language, of course, is an integral part of communication. How integral, you might wonder? Take a closer look.

Personal Relationships

Body language affect and influences personal relationships, sometimes deliberately and sometimes spontaneous. Think about the last time you went to dinner with a special someone - what kinds of body language did you use to communicate affection, interest, and the like?

In the same vein, think about sitting down in a business meeting next to another person whom you do not particularly like. What kind of body language did you use to maintain a polite business demeanor without expressing levels of friendship you did not genuinely feel?

Professional And Business Endeavors

Body language has a great deal to do with how you perform

and how you are perceived in the business world. Perhaps the most obvious application is in sales and customer service, where body language is an active part of working with clients and customers to solicit and maintain their business.

For instance, how well would you do as a customer service agent if you consistently frowned, turned away from customers, and generally showed body language indicating you really did not care?

Parenting

Body language is a huge part of parenting, both in how you communicate with your children and how you interpret their communication with you. Babies and infants obviously use a great deal of body language since they cannot speak, but so do toddlers and pre-school aged children. Have you ever seen a toddler throw him- or herself to the ground in a fit or tantrum? That is powerful body language indeed.

□□

Chapter 15

Communication within the Organization

ORGANIZATIONAL COMMUNICATION

Communication is context dependent and draws on many social sources of meaning other than the content of a given message or series of messages. Sources of meaning may include very broad socio-political factors, such as, the type of society in which it occurs. Let us review the role and function of communication in three broad types of societies: preliterate, modern, and postmodern. Some aspects of postmodernism as a context for communicational analysis are discussed.

Communication in Context

The aim here is to compare the quality, function, and consequences of dominant forms of communication in different socio cultural contexts. This outline will provide the reader with a rudimentary understanding of selected similarities and differences found between preliterate, modern, and postmodern societies. The three societies are presented as *ideal types*, or selected, abstracted, idealized versions of societies in which certain features of analytic interest become the basis for the comparisons. The simplest and most basic point to be made is that size brings within it changes in the division of labour, social differentiation, and changes in the frequency, quality, and character of communications. In short, communication changes from face-to-face to some combination of face to face and mass communications. In postmodern society, tertiary or media-mediated experiences become the most common and salient. In this sense, the social types presented capture correlates of and changes in the nature of communication.

Changes in Communication in Types of Societies

Preliterate Societies

- Dense and closely articulated social relations.
- Shared symbols and symbolic repertoires.
- Roles are simpler (few sources, role signs) and sign vehicles are known and local.
- Social control is consistent and determined by many institutions.
- Intimate relations, family and kin relations, and ascribed statuses are key to ordering.
- Ecologically bounded and defined.
- Economically self-sufficient.
- Non industrial roles predominate.
- Money is absent.
- Communicational channels are shared.
- Networks are known, face-to-face communication is prevalent.
- Mass communications are absent.
- Bureaucracies are absent.
- Authenticity, authority, and the sacred coalesce.
  - Secular knowledge legitimates meanings.
  - Moral codes and boundaries are messy, and not well understood; moral categories are vaguely shared.
- Sacred canopy of religion defines ultimate truths and dominates.
- Social and moral boundaries are clear and well-understood; moral categories are shared.

Modern Industrial Societies

- Social relations are loosely linked.
- Non shared symbols and symbolic repertoires exist.
- Roles and sign vehicles are both local and national.
- Social control is narrowly defined and often formally determined.
- Intimate relations are embedded in diffuse and loose networks of acquaintances.
- Class, race, and achieved statuses are key to social ordering.
- Bureaucratic (service-based) work is central.
- Ecological boundaries are diffuse; national boundaries are salient.
- Knowledge production is valued (science, R and D, intelligence).
- Money is the great zero symbol having all possible meanings and none at all.

Postmodern Societies

- Social relations are keyed by media.
- Symbols are shared as media mediated.
- Roles and sign vehicles are visual, distant, and artificial (created).
- Social control is reflected in media and weakly articulated.
- Non intimate relations rise in centrality in shaping identity and self; family, kin, and other ascribed statuses are less likely to key ordering.
- Media societies are ecologically unbounded; symbolically entail experience of world events as "personal."
- *Simulacra* (images) are both creators and created of the desirable; the real is that which is capable of reproduction.

- Economically interdependent (individually and nationally).
- Work and leisure roles are in tension.
- Money is the great zero symbol, signifying all possible meanings and none at all.

- Shared communicational channels and networks are known; face-to-face and larger, looser sets of mass communication networks key meaning and experience.
- Bureaucracies are work settings for most.
- Authenticity, authority, and the sacred coalesce.
  - Secular knowledge legitimates meanings.
  - Moral codes and boundaries are messy, and not well understood; moral categories are vaguely shared.
- Secular meanings dominate.
- Moral codes and boundaries are messy, and not well-understood; moral categories are vaguely shared.

Having laid out these these types, we are now positioned to ask what sorts of communications are characteristic of the emergent postmodern society, and how this postmodern view of the future differs from an alternative vision of the future.

COMMUNICATION AND GROUP DISCUSSION

Getting Feedback

Get "feedback". Have the employee play back your ideas, information, or instruction in his own words. If he says what you meant to say, your communication effort was successful. But if he errs' there has been a flaw in sending, in receiving, or both. You then repeat this process until the employee sees what you see. This technique used in oral communication is a virtually foolproof method of putting the "see" into communication. It is standard operating procedure in the U.S. Army Infantry to get such feedback on all oral field orders, and there is no doubt that this procedure has saved many lives in battle.

Save The Employee's Face

When you criticize, do so privately. Make your criticism constructive by showing the employee a better way. Always direct your comments to the employee's work and not to him personally.

Recognize The Employee's Progress

Compliment him/her on his good work and, at the same time, encourage him to strive for even greater achievement.

A Feeling Of Belonging

One of our strongest desires is to belong and to be accepted by a group or groups. Man is undeniably a social animal. Aristotle once said, "a man who lives outside society is either a god or beast." This feeling of belonging, however, is not acquired by nominal membership in a group. It is acquired by participation.

Participation

Participation by the individual's contributing something of value to the group's work, and by the group's recognizing the contribution as worthwhile. Communication can do much to satisfy the desire to belong in two ways:

- ***Consultative Management:*** First, each supervisor should consult with his subordinates before instituting changes in processes, personnel, or equipment, a practice known as consultative management.

  Supervisors should make it a habit to ask their employees what they think, then listen and get their ideas. Whenever you ask someone, "What do you think?", you flatter him. You say to him, in effect, "I value your judgment." Not only does this approach raise employee morale and strengthen supervisor employee rapport, but it often opens the floodgates to a flow of valuable ideas which can increase efficiency and cut costs. Every supervisor should he mindful of the fact that no one is quite as conversant with the details of a job as the man who does it daily. Many employees get good ideas from time to time about improving their jobs.

These ideas should be tapped. Consultative management is particularly important when changes an contemplated. Most of us tend to resist change. We have adapted ourselves, sometimes painfully, to the status quo, and we dislike having the pattern of our lives upset, especially when changes come abruptly and unexpectedly.

- ***Frequent Use Of Group Problem Solving:*** Second, each level of management *should make more frequent use of group problem solving*. Group problem solving meetings have one merit, perhaps their greatest, which is often overlooked or glossed over. This merit is the tremendous lift which this method can give a group's morale, for this is participation at its best. In addition to the morale factor, such meetings provide an ideal milieu for horizontal communication, for the rapid exchange of ideas between supervisors across departmental lines. Such exchanges promote mutual understanding, enhance cooperation and coordination of effort, and knit the players of the company team more closely together.

Inducing Cooperation

To induce your employees to accept change cooperatively and to introduce it as smoothly as possible, get them to participate whenever practicable in planning and implementing it. If you do this, they will probably produce a number of valuable ideas that never occurred to you, ideas that will make the change better for all concerned. But, best of all, they will support the change because they had a hand in it. It is their change, a product of their effort. In addition to their participation, it is important that all employees affected by an impending change clearly see how they will individually and collectively benefit from it. Satisfy their desire to know what is in it for them.

Emotional Security

Few conditions contribute more to a sense of emotional security than being employed by a well-managed organization.

All of us like order and predictability. We like to know what we can and cannot do. We like to know how we are doing. And we like to feel that we can predict fairly accurately where we are going. In companies having good communication between management and employees, the employees know these things, for, in such companies, employees are well trained and well informed; jurisdictional lines are carefully drawn; each employee knows what he is supposed to do, where, when, how, and why he is supposed to do it; penalties for poor performance are firm, fair, and clearly understood; and credit for good work is freely and promptly give".

In summary, communication is the conveyance of meaning designed to motivate people to take desired action. People act most readily to satisfy their wants. Communication is the principal means by which the supervisor can help his employees satisfy their job-related wants. Communication, therefore, is the supervisor's most important tool.

Study Of Diversity Personnel

At a micro level a focus group study of diversity personnel and an interview based study of mid-level managers, from two different units of a large investment banking firm, provide a snapshot of the attitudes and perceptions of personnel in a white-collar industry that espouses a commitment to diversity programming. The units in these studies are a part of one of the oldest American investment banking institutions, and it has historically been a leader that defined the nature of that business. As such, the firm conveys and maintains an image that has developed over a rich history. The image of being a leader in the investment banking industry has been exceptionally important to the firm. It defines itself as a world-class company operating in the fast-moving, highly competitive financial services marketplace, and realises that it must attract, keep and develop the very best people. The CEO explains that: "We are building for the next generation, not the next transaction. To do this we must be an undisputed employer of choice." The firm appears to be committed to developing and maintaining diversity at every level of the company.

The data in this study was gathered over a period of three months with the conduct of six one-half-day focus groups. Each focus group was composed of a group of approximately ten members of the banking group that provides financial services to businesses. The focus group participants were selected because they fit into a protected category, i.e. historically minority status. Consequently this sample included the minority personnel and a cross-section of female personnel and represented approximately 10 per cent of the employees in this nationwide unit of the bank. This sample was intended to be inclusive of diversity personnel in order to focus on airing all the major issues that concerned these protected groups. Personnel were brought to the focus group location from across the United States. Two focus groups were conducted in Princeton, New Jersey, and four groups were conducted in Chicago.

The executive in charge of the financial services business unit that the focus groups were drawn from made a point of coming to each group and expressed his support for the diversity management project and this fact-finding research. Participants were impressed with his support. This was a key element to making the focus groups successful. It is clear that visible executive support is an essential element for success.

The participants in the diversity focus groups seemed to appreciate the cathartic experience of talking about a subject that they had some uncertainty about. Many lacked even a basic knowledge of the diversity mission of their corporation. Several said they 'never expected to have an opportunity to discuss these sensitive issues'.

There were no major complaints that could be labeled as unique to this corporate unit. Some participants, who had worked in other units of the firm reported that this unit was much more diversity friendly than their previous group. Although this was a long-standing unit of more than six hundred members, there have been no catalytic events in recent memory in the unit that would serve as a flash point for concern over diversity. The incidents reported by the participants were generally not egregious nor widely discussed by co-workers. The negative incidents seemed to be considered as isolated incidents and not representative of the attitudes and behaviour of the majority of unit personnel.

Most of the persons in the focus groups were quite ignorant of what their company had done or not done with diversity initiatives. They had queries for information and in a sense the focus groups became a form of action research because the participants' questions were answered and they received new information on what was happening. Action research has become 'increasingly prominent' in the study of organizations when they indicate it is: 'research which broadly, results from an involvement by the researcher with members of an organization over a matter which is of genuine concern to them and in which there is an intent by the organization members to take action based on the intervention'.

Developing and conducting the focus groups was a prelude to further action research. It should be noted that this focus group process was a catalyst for an evolving diversity initiative that included the establishment of a 'diversity council' to suggest and monitor future actions. In this way the participants had a sense of outcome from the focus group project. Affirmative action was a frequent, but not particularly comfortable subject in these groups. They appreciate the goals of affirmative action but it can produce a somewhat uncomfortable paradox. All of the participants believe that the firm hired them because of their skill and experience. To these personnel endorsing affirmative action might connote that their hiring may have been the result of some preference. Most of these people indicate that if in a pool of equally qualified candidates there is a minority, at this point in the history of firm, the minority person should be selected. Focus group participants emphatically express the position that 'no one should ever be hired who cannot do the job'. Discussants often mentioned the fact that traditional methods of recruiting may not reach many persons who could be in a qualified minority pool. It was frequently noted that investment banking is dominated and staffed almost completely by white males. The dynamic in the groups was stimulating because participants were eager to make constructive action proposals. The following is a list of major suggestions made by the focus group participants. They are included in no particular order, but represent the major reactions of the sixty participants:

- Work to maintain respect, regardless of gender, ethnicity, or race.
- Maintain commitment to diversity and work to increase heterogeneity.
- To assume that the whole group has a problem is not fair. Don't try to fix what is not broken. Get in with the workforce and fix the real problems that are there.
- Provide meaningful diversity training. This should be a part of the orientation process for new employees. Continually reinforce the principles and behaviours taught in the training.
- Managers must be well and extensively trained in diversity management.
- The managers' performance review should include how well they manage diversity. This task of reinforcement and maintenance of effective diversity management falls upon the managers and the respective styles that they model for everyone else in the group.
- The firm needs to do a better job of performance reviews. Managers need to do a better job of letting you know what to do to get promoted. Help us with what we need to learn and accomplish so that we perform more effectively.
- In the interest of trying to promote diverse people, don't just promote people because of their diversity status, forgetting their qualifications. Don't put someone somewhere just to have a minority in that position.
- Career planning is important to everyone. Career counseling and advising is important and it should be done. This could solve some of the problem we have with a high turnover rate. The people we tend to lose will be minorities who have excellent opportunities elsewhere. What are their opportunities here? They need to know.

- As this unit grows we need to do more mentoring. It is essential to have more training and mentoring for those who want to move up to management.
- This unit must deal more effectively with the problem of attrition. If we lowered the attrition rate there would be fewer personnel problems.
- As a matter of course do exit interviews and listen to them. Learn from the reasons people leave.
- Improve recruiting - go beyond putting advertisements in the paper. Be more visible at career fairs. Go to a wider range of universities to recruit.
- Take time while hiring. Don't do it too quickly. 'Emergency hires' can't be done carefully. Go slow and get somebody really good for the job. Go past the typical criteria for hiring. Only using referrals won't accomplish the diversity goals. Instead of looking at educational background, look at their talent. Look creatively at the past history of candidates' work. Even though I am at a lower level let me do some hiring or at least be more involved in the hiring process.
- Maintain, embrace and apply more of the quality of work-life policies that the firm brags about. Don't offer policies, if managers don't intend to use them. Walk the talk.
- Establish a diversity council and define what it will do. It's not going to work to just talk about diversity. This group should be very active.
- Get individual groups of particular minority categories together for sessions like this. Blacks, Asians, women, etc. See if they have more ideas to share when they are only with persons with the same category. If you want to get to the truth, do this to get a definite sense of the peer groups.
- Do a quarterly newsletter that highlights diversity features, and initiatives. If it is put online attach it in an easy to find and read manner. Overall we are in a

growth mode and we need to be able to get to know the new people.

- Report to us. We want to hear the results of what the groups said in these focus groups.

Study Of Mid-level Managers

The sessions focused both on information gathering and coaching the managers. The second study that provides a view of the attitudes and perceptions of personnel in a white-collar industry of investment banking is based upon a focused set of ninety-minute interviews with twenty-five mid-level managers in the mutual funds division of the firm. This again was a form of action research because the interview provided an opportunity to conduct a constructive dialogue on some of the issues of concern to the interviewees. The focus of the interviews was on both the process of evaluation and the impact of dealing with a diverse workforce. Topics included discovery of diversity sensitivity, coaching people through difficult performance evaluation sessions, working for candour, honesty, openness in performance management sessions, maintaining a climate that is non-defensive, and the general problems the supervisors faced in dealing with those who reported to them. The performance evaluation issues reported by the managers were as follows:

- Adapting performance appraisals to different types of people is a challenging process. Many are not sure of how their perceptions fit within the context of the cultural background of those who come from very different cultures.
- It would be beneficial to receive more feedback regarding the nature of my leadership style. I'm not sure how it fits a range of different people.
- Dealing with someone who used to be a peer and now I am her/his boss.
- Discussing issues that are team issues with individuals.
- Working to define clear and measurable critical objectives.

- How to continue to motivate someone who is evaluated as an exceptional performer. Helping them to see how they can add value.
- How to motivate people who are in a dead-end job.
- Understanding the motivation, or lack thereof, of the new generation of staff.
- How to sincerely communicate a positive sense of morale to persons who have low morale.

In this sample group the managers also had concerns about their personal performance for which they sought discussion and advice:

- Finding ways to get better feedback from my boss.
- Giving my boss feedback about how he/she provides feedback to me.
- Working on personal impression management and knowing how to 'build your skills and your personal franchise'.
- Communication/leadership aspects of forming a new team.
- How to reinforce and maintain the communication things I am doing that are effective with my team.
- How to encourage the culture to open up the conversations? Can we motivate by other than fear?
- How to approach further personal development as a supervisor.
- Dealing with cross-cultural communication differences.
- Managing meetings.

COMMUNICATION BEGINS AT THE TOP

Communication must be an integral and vital part of management's philosophy. As all management philosophies, it must originate with top management and be a continuing network for the exchange of information and ideas up, down, and across the company structure. It must be as much a part of management planning as production schedules, procurement of materials, and the maintenance of equipment. And it must function continuously, not just when a crisis occurs. Management, therefore, must be communication conscious at all times.

This does not mean that supervisors should bare their souls to their employees or completely divulge every decision and plan, but it does mean that every supervisor should consider the advisability of complete disclosure with due regard to the limitations applicable to his situation. And if something should be told, the supervisor must, of course, decide when, where, to whom, and how.

While any plant-wide or company-wide communication programme must start at the top and radiate downward through every echelon of management, the first. Line supervisor is the key in any continuing communication programme. He is the king-pin who can unite or sunder the labour management segments of the company team. To the worker, he personifies the company, and it is he who is the key link in most upward communication from worker to top management. Likewise, it is he who must interpret company policy to the worker, pass on information, and transmit orders and instructions.

Up to this point, we have considered only the vertical half of the communication function. It is equally important, however, that ideas and information be communicated across the company structure as it is that they be communicated up and down. This means that management personnel at each level must view themselves as links in a horizontal chain of communication.

No matter how effective a company's vertical communication may be, if its supervisors are not communicating well with each other and if they do not know, understand, and accept each other's problems and needs, there can be only ineffectual teamwork and poor cooperation.

ELIMINATING COMMUNICATION ROADBLOCKS

How can interdepartmental barriers to communication and understanding he overcome? The best and quickest way is by frequent face-to-face discussions at each level of management, provided such discussions are approached with an open mind and a spirit of friendly helpfulness. Such interdepartmental discussions should be aimed primarily at exchanging knowledge, creating understanding, and gaining acceptance of each other's problems and needs. These meetings should take place as often as practicable until each supervisor is so thoroughly familiar with and appreciative of the needs and problems of his peers that he consistently and unhesitatingly coordinates his efforts with theirs.

A second and equally formidable, communication roadblock is the barrier of status and position.

It particularly; inhibits the flow of upward communication. Some men "freeze up" in the presence of their superiors and experience mental blocks which prevent them from expressing themselves fully or clearly. Other men take the position that "what the boss doesn't know won't hurt him" and deliberately screen out all unpleasant information which might upset their superiors. Often these self-appointed censors screen out information that management urgently needs to function intelligently.

What can management do to "thaw out" its employees, to put them at ease, and gel them to "open up"? The first and most important step is to establish by the daily example of top management a free and permissive climate favouring upward communication. Once this climate has been established at the top, it will quickly permeate the entire organization.

There are two intangible but essential elements in a good communication climate: an attitude that is people-centred rather than production-centred and an open door in fact as well as in word.

This is not an atmosphere that can he established by words, but only by deeds, by management's daily example on the job. Besides practicing what It preaches, management must make It clear to all supervisors that they should make time for communication. The driving insistence that every moment of a supervisor's time be spent on production is too frequently the preoccupation of some top managers. Such thinking has no place in modern management, for experience had abundantly demonstrated that the supervisor's job is handling people and that devoting enough time to communicating with them is an integral and inescapable part of that job.

Is there one best way of communicating? Not for all situations and messages, but face-to-face communication is preferable whenever it is practicable. It is personal and warmer than other media. It can convey more meaning than written or telephonic communication, because the parties can also communicate via gestures and facial expressions. It is quick and inexpensive. It permits immediate feedback and clarification. When each level of management communicates with the next lower level by meetings, three distinct benefits accrue:

- Management's leadership at each level will be strengthened by regularly scheduled, face-to-face meetings.
- The information conveyed at such meetings will usually be much more complete and accurate than that transmitted on the grapevine.
- The workers will look increasingly to their supervisors rather than the union or the grapevine for company information.

SUMMARY AND CONCLUSION

Management is *man management*. As Lawrence Appley has said, "Management is personnel administration." The results managers get can be achieved only through people. Since the supervisor cannot slave drive people for a prolonged period without having it backfire, he must motivate them affirmatively by the carrot rather than the stick. A good communication programme is a powerful motivational influence, because it makes it possible for employees to satisfy many of their basic wants, such as recognition, communication, belonging, and emotional security.

Communication activities contributing to the satisfaction of these needs are induction, training, coaching, counseling, listening, informational meetings, consultative management, and group problem solving.

The cardinal prerequisite for a successful communication programme is a proper climate. This must first be established at the top-management level, from which it will radiate downward throughout the entire organization. To sustain this climate, management must be employee centered, keep an open door, listen, and allow time for communication. Finally, all persons in the organization with important communication responsibilities should be located and trained in the most effective use of communication skills.

Removing barriers to communication, establishing a favourable communication climate, and improving the supervisor's skills as a communicator are among the foremost challenges and opportunities facing modern management. One of the measures of an organization's success is the extent to which its management has recognized and met this challenge.

□□

Chapter 16

Readability in Written Communication

Most working professionals, particularly those in middle and upper management, routinely produce a variety of messages, many of which are in the written form of memoranda, electronic mail, letters, reports, performance reviews, instructions, procedures, and proposals. Yet when these messages are judged according to the intentions of the writers, they traditionally fall into just two categories of writing: persuasive and informative.

Of the two, persuasive writing is much more demanding because it attempts to bring about an important change in the reader's beliefs or actions. Thus writing persuasively requires giving considerable attention to a resistant reader, one who can be expected to challenge the writer's efforts. Writing persuasively also requires examining not only one's own beliefs but also the reasons one holds them and the reasons others do not. Because this form of writing is so demanding, and because it is usually recognized as the most advanced form of composition. Here we will look at a preparatory task: informative writing. Writing informatively is the working professional's most frequent writing task, one that has an oral counterpart in voice mail and impromptu speaking. Informative writing often takes the form of a memo, letter, or e-mail message, though sometimes a longer report or analysis will serve as the vehicle for presentation. Since informative messages can be about almost any topic, writers cannot use the content of a message to distinguish informative from persuasive messages. Compounding the problem of identifying the informative message is the fact that no message is purely informative.

Each message is a mixture of intentions to inform and persuade. Nevertheless, an important distinguishing feature of informative writing is a reader who is easier to satisfy than the resistant reader of persuasive messages. By definition, readers of informative messages do not resist the writer, primarily because they do not feel that the writer has a controversial point of view. Because these readers do not appear as adversaries, writers can and usually do treat informative writing as if it existed without any serious competition. But nor do they feel that the writer has a vested interest in overcoming their opposing point of view or the contrary interests of others.

COMMUNICATION IN BUSINESS

This resistance is the product of two conflicting forces in modern business: the rapidly increasing rate at which information is produced and disseminated and the dramatically decreasing amount of time the working reader has to spend on it. Writers need to understand this resistance and the conflicting forces that help to produce it. Nevertheless, writers routinely run into trouble because they do not understand that informative writing is in fact competitive. And it is competitive because of the kind of resistance that characterizes readers in the professions. The rate at which information is produced and disseminated has been the topic of many studies. Most of us know we are in the midst of an information explosion, one that continues to be fueled by rapid advances in technology. While this is true of the world in which we all live, it is especially true for the world of business. Of all the professions, business is the primary consumer of technology and information, and a recognition of this underlies major studies of modern business culture, and even predictions about a new kind of product — information — and a new kind of worker, "the knowledge worker".

Business will probably only increase its consumption of information. Those who have studied changes in the work force over the next decade argue that a cultural shift will continue to take place, one that will result in a greater sharing of information in the corporate setting. Along with the increase in the sharing of information will be a new attitude of seriousness adopted toward messages that were previously viewed as peripheral. Newsletters, for example, will become more substantial carriers of important information. Thus, business will most probably increase not only its consumption of information but also the attention it is asked to pay to it. Unfortunately, these developments come at a time when readers and other receivers of information have less time than ever before. Changes in the structure of the modern business organization, drastic and widespread downsizing, and increased competition have all reduced the time the manager was once able to devote to written messages. Readers in business can no longer afford to review material at relative leisure, and those who once had information processed for them in summaries, abstracts, or executive briefings find that they must now do it themselves. As a consequence, many are developing techniques for "scanning" information, a phenomenon that has only recently received the attention of those who study communication. They are becoming more selective of the messages they read even as those messages compete more fully for their attention.

What writers need to appreciate about these recent and predicted developments is this: modern readers in business have to manage significantly more information than ever before, and they have significantly less time to spend on it. These are conflicting forces, but they are also *competing* forces, since they contend powerfully for the reader's attention. In practice, this means that writers will have to adopt special strategies for presentation, strategies that acknowledge the reader's resistance as well as the competing forces of increased information and decreased time.

Overcoming this resistance can take many forms. For instance, writers could attempt to reduce the number of documents they produce, or not even write at all. This is probably a prudent course of action, at least in its tempered form, simply because the fewer the documents, the more attention they will receive as a matter of novelty. However, it is not a solution, even in its more tempered form, and writers who choose to produce fewer documents will find that the information may well need to be communicated in other, sometimes more time-consuming and less effective ways. They will also find that their reluctance to write can result in forfeiting their place of participation, record, and influence in the information community.

COMPETITION AND ORGANIZATION

Organization, or *disposition,* as it was called in classical rhetoric, is a powerful and time-honored solution to problems that result from increased information and decreased time. Although writers cannot meet resistance with reluctance, they can meet it with something else: organization. Without organization, readers will not be inclined to follow the writer from point to point and will not be able to retain the writer's message. In fact, the frustration and despair that can result from not being able to follow disorganized messages is only now becoming clear in the very publications that concern themselves with information.

For example, in one issue of *PC Magazine,* chief editor Bill Macron offered telling observations on his experience at a conference with a theme that "ignores the here and now in order to look farther down the road at the events and technologies that will shape the industry in the coming years":

Here, information is presented as a force that will require "tools to organize" it if it is to have meaning. Unfortunately, Macron continued by discussing one of these tools, one of his "favourite approaches to the information glut". This new software product possessed "a parsing engine that understands sentences and parts of speech." With the addition of considerable memory on disk, this programme was supposed to be able to "extract the meaning and most important ideas from unstructured text."

Macron certainly understood the importance of organization, though he may be a bit optimistic about the capability of software programmes to produce it and thereby reveal meaning. However, good writers do just that. They provide their readers with "the meaning and most important ideas" when they organize their informative messages. By providing their readers with an organized message, writers can offer the promise of efficient reading and clear understanding. By consistently providing organized messages, writers can begin to earn a reputation for producing documents that are distinctive in quality and therefore appeal. Thus writers can gain an advantage over the forces that lead to resistance and thereby compete for their readers' attention. Unfortunately, organization does not characterize business writing. This may be surprising to some simply because organization in many matters — personnel, finance, investment- is strongly associated with the business enterprise. The popularity of software schedulers, project managers, and personal information managers suggests that organization is highly valued in most areas of practical business activity. Yet other evidence suggests that writing in business is no more and perhaps even less organized than writing done elsewhere. The task is then, to discuss organization and its application to informative writing in business.

Organization And Arrangement

Understanding what organization is requires understanding what it is not, particularly in business writing. When asked how they organize their writing, working professionals in one long-term survey responded in ways that suggest they don't organize their writing at all. Some never responded, and others who did respond candidly admitted that they simply do not organize their writing. Of those who did see themselves organizing their writing, most indicated that they organized while they were writing or that they worked from a list of points.

Since the writers who said they work from a list of points came the closest to providing any form of organization, this approach bears some comment. It also bears comment because of the prevalence of lists and listing devices in business writing. The listing device appears to provide organization but does not. Even though it's alphabetical, numerical, or bulleted presentation may be familiar to the reader, a simple list only *appears* to organize. In a list that is presented numerically, the number 2 certainly follows the number 1, just as the letter B follows A in the alphabetized version. However, nothing about the numerical or alphabetical version will show important relationships within the information the list contains. This is also true of the traditional college outline, which is essentially a listing device, and report headings that are used to increase readability. Simple lists, headings, and outlines *are* easy to read, and they should be used for that very reason, but this does not mean they provide organization to the material they contain. If listing devices do not provide organization, we may well ask what does. Organization comes not from the *listing* of information but from the *arranging* of it. Because of that, we will come to expect two things from an organized document: first, that the arrangement of its parts be apparent; second, that the arrangement have an underlying principle that unites the parts of the arrangement. The difference between a list and an arrangement is illustrated by the following two simple examples. Each represents a kind of organization from which the writer intends to write. The topic concerns purchasing computers by direct mail:

1. Some people have used it.
2. Experience has been mixed.
3. Many people may become skeptical about it.
4. Past opinions
5. Present opinions
6. Future opinions

Comparing the lists will usually result in a preference for the second, and most people will feel intuitively that the second is better organized simply because the items have words in common, and the pattern of repetition probably suggests greater design. The second is in fact better organized, though explaining why another matter is. Still, we can usually explain organization by testing for it. To do this, we remove the list's cosmetics, the numbers, letters, or bullets that stand before the information that will be developed. If we do that with the first example, nothing appears to unite the items, and no arrangement is *evident*. However, if we do it with the second example, we find that each has something evidently in common with the others, the *principle* of time. We could even present a reader with the first two ("past and present opinions") and reasonably expect the reader to predict the third ("future opinions") because the principle of organization would suggest it. Thus, organization exists as a principled and evident arrangement.

Such organization also exists as a critically important link between writer and reader because the principle behind the organization — time, balance, place, etc. — is one that *the reader brings to the reading experience.* Since the writer and reader both recognize this pattern of organization, it will serve them as a map they can travel along together. The writer *and* reader need to acknowledge the principle of time if they are both to move without confusion from past to present to future. Of course, knowing what organization is and does tells us nothing about where it comes from or how to select among different organizational options. Not many who study communication have written about this, and only a few have written about it in any detail. Furthermore, the advice, which represents much of the conventional thinking in this area, is probably not the best to follow.

The first step in successful planning is a consideration of organizations with a view to eliminating those unsuited to the material. This selection is usually simple. A writer rejects chronological order if there is no time sequence in his subject, geographical divisions if his topic has none, and climactic order if his main ideas have no suitable variations in importance. Second, a thoughtful writer considers his readers and does his best to select the organization that will be most helpful to them. This choice may involve more deliberation than does the selection of a plan suitable to the material, but it is not necessarily more difficult. While the content of this advice is good, it is backwards; at least it is for business applications. The first step is not oriented toward the interests of the reader, and the second step may well make the first one redundant or nonsensical. Since much that is written in business is solicited, this advice neglects the initial and important role the reader can play in helping the writer determine the appropriate organization, which ultimately is the organization that provides the reader with the kind of information the *reader* needs.

The guidelines that follow consider the reader in just this way, as the primary influence on choice of organization. These guidelines provide a systematic approach to informative writing, one that is particularly sensitive to the reader's resistance. They also present an organized approach, one that covers the writer's responsibilities *before, during,* and *after* writing.

Before Composing

A significant amount of business writing is solicited by others, and the solicitation will often imply a way of organizing a written response. Because of this, writers will want to read or listen to their solicitations very carefully. Many of our personnel are urging us to move to flextime. Look into this; let me know what has caused them to feel this way, and what will happen if we go to flextime. Although this is less straightforward, a careful reading will help the writer discern the structure. Two phrases in particular, "what has caused" and "what will happen" show the writer that the supervisor is interested in the *causes* and *effects* of going to flextime, and the writer can use this form of organization to frame a response.

When the request implies a form of organization, the writer should seriously consider using it because it helps to insure that the response is well organized and that the response will satisfy the reader's request. Much of the time, though, the request will be so vague and unhelpful that it implies nothing about how a written response might be organized. For example, an e-mail message might say the following:

"I just read the Chronicle piece on our contractors in Sunnyvale. What gives?"

In this case, and in cases where writing is *not* requested, the writer may well wonder what to do about organization. Several options are available. First, the writer can use prior knowledge about the reader to select an appropriate form of organization. If the reader has a known preference for balanced reviews, the writer may well select an organization of balance. If the reader usually expects information to have background as well as prediction, the writer may want to use some form of chronological organization. If the writer simply has *no idea* what the reader may want, a quick telephone call or question on e-mail may help. Often a question that proposes a form of organization is best because it gives the reader something to accept or reject. At worst, the writer will know what the reader *does not* want, and that will help to determine what *is* needed. Should the writer be entirely unable to determine a form of organization appropriate to the reader, then turning to the subject matter for direction would make good sense. In either case, the writer will need to accept the responsibility for organizing the writing. Without a form of organization, the writer will lack direction, and the reader will be less able to follow and retain the information the letter, memo, or report contains.

□□

Chapter 17

Emotional Intelligence

THE KEY TO EMOTIONAL INTELLIGENCE

Emotional Intelligence (EI) is the ability to sense, understand, and effectively apply the power of emotions, appropriately channeled as a source of energy, creativity and influence - and to be able to clear and release emotions which have outstayed their welcome. Sometimes, for most of us, we may be afraid to face our deepest feelings, needs and thoughts.

We may be afraid to express them to another because of how we imagine the other may react. So we live private lives, partly cut off from partners, friends, colleagues and family, and even from ourselves.

A wall of frustration or emotional 'charge' develops between two people (or between a person and an organization) when what is felt is not expressed, or what is expressed is not listened to with understanding and empathy.

HOW DOES EI MAKE A DIFFERENCE AND HOW DO WE USE IT?

Tips on Cultivating More Emotional Intelligence and Better Communication Skills:

- When colleagues, friends and relatives choose to confide in you about their feelings and thoughts don't shy away. Instead of interpreting their display of courage as a weakness, use it as important information and insight into this person's life and your relationship with them. You may discover things about them you never knew.

- Even if you are feeling threatened by another person's strengths, avoid the temptation to think of ways to sabotage them and instead try to think about how or why they do what they do. What motivates them? What background do they have that leads them to be noticed the way they are? Compliment them on their strengths.
- Lots of mistakes are made when we assume the behaviour of others as meaning something that it may not, e.g. a sideways glance or failing to acknowledge a question. Did the other fail to hear us or are they pulling some kind of power play? The only way to know for sure is to ask! Don't project your own thoughts onto them. Go ahead and check in. Ask if you've misinterpreted something. If their behaviour was petty – they'll be alerted that you know what they are up to and if not – you will have cleared something up that could snowball for years. But be ready to be surprised – truly listen to their answer – tone of voice, body language, and all.
- Is what I said what you heard? When assignments are given out or agreements made – repeat and follow-up on them. Ask about how someone feels about her work. This isn't to baby-sit them – it's to find out what kind of work the other person likes and thinks they are good at. Tell them that so they don't assume that you are being condescending or competitive. You could waste years developing bad rapport with a direct report thinking that you are helping them out. Not all *"help"* is good help. If you tune in accurately – you could gain valuable loyalty for the rest of your career! Not everyone who is talented wants to be a leader – and many do cherish good leaders when they find them.
- When you say something – mean it. One person with integrity is worth perhaps a thousand whose words

mean nothing. Make others feel comfortable talking to you. Tell them you appreciate what they've told you and share a few of your own experiences. These seemingly unimportant things could lead to worthwhile ideas and collaborations on future projects unforeseen in the present.

- Don't wait for upper management to notice how important your emotionally intelligent skills are – quantify them! Tell them how conflict was avoided, problems solved, morale uplifted and productivity increased.

  Get data to back it up. Better yet, start a group of emotionally intelligent co-workers within your company or department and back one another up. Numbers always count!

HOW TO DEAL WITH THOSE WITHOUT EI?

The tips above will help you develop your own skills regarding emotional intelligence and you will be able to evaluate those around you who have it, and those who don't. What do you do about those who don't have a high EI? Here are a few suggestions:

- If you are responsible for hiring, do not put people who seem to be lacking in emotional intelligence in a position where they are responsible for other people.

  Not only will the department suffer and those that work underneath these people, but you could be opening up the company to potential lawsuits, bad publicity or worse. We've all read in the papers about people who have abused their authority – a good majority of them have very low emotional acumen.

- Do not try to change or expect someone to develop emotional skills if they show no desire or ability in this area. Some people truly don't know what it is they are missing. Find out what skills they are good at and give them more assignments in this area. Recognize those successes in a way that they want to be recognized.

- If you find a co-worker reacting to something in an undesirable way, ask them how they interpreted the situation – don't assume that there is something wrong with them or with their competence or anything else. Many times what seems like a mountain is actually a molehill and can be cleared up in minutes with some perspective.

Bringing some emotional intelligence into the workplace isn't a sign that a boardroom meeting will turn into a therapy session. Rather, it signals a new wave of worker, leader, and workplace environment that recognizes that key communication skills, and emotional intelligence lead to better business.

□□

Chapter 18

Communication on Telephone

For years, Support Centre managers have been tasked with maintaining and improving the high-tech skills of the Support Centre staff. *High-tech skills*, mean product knowledge and problem-solving skills. These skills are vital since the primary task of support agents is to solve customers' technical problems. In recent years, however, the importance of *high-touch skills* has become more fully recognized. *High-touch skills* or communication skills, are primarily speaking and listening skills.

THE CUSTOMER RELATIONSHIP COMPOSITED

Figure above shows a model called the "customer relationship composite." In this composite, you'll see the various skills that influence interactions with customers. Speaking skills and listening skills represent the two high-touch needs, while problem-solving skills and product knowledge represent the two high-tech needs. All the components function in a two-way manner. In other words, both the agent and the customer exhibit all four skills. The agent is not the only one who has product knowledge and problem-solving skills—in fact, a good

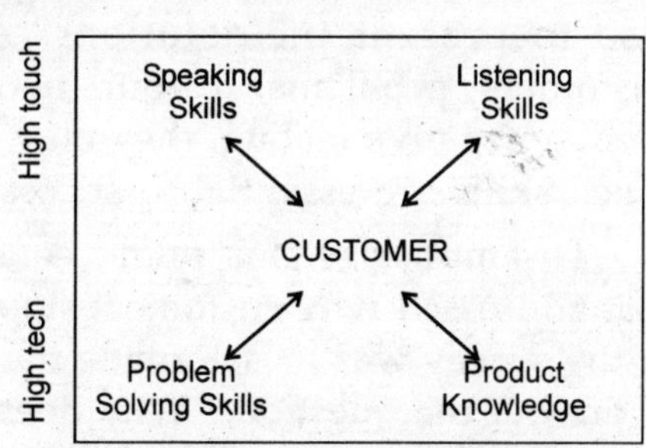

Fig. 1. The customer relationship composite shows the various influences in our relationships with customers.

agent will draw upon these resources that the customer brings to the relationship. Naturally, this information is drawn out from the customer using speaking and listening skills.

When both parties bring strong skills to the service request, the interaction can be an efficient and rewarding exchange of valuable information. Imagine each of these skills as the legs of a table. If during any customer interaction one of these legs should falter, the table will collapse.

That might sound severe, but think about it. Product knowledge and problem solving skills are essential. Even if you have to call the customer back or refer the problem to a second level agent, your Support Centre must be able to own the service request until it is resolved. The Help Desk or Support Centre must have a strong resource of high-tech skills to draw from because most of the solutions are technical in nature.

If in the end you don't have the high-tech skills, the interaction will be unsuccessful. So maintaining these skills at your organization is essential. However, the high-touch skills are also vital. As an agent, you need to communicate with customers to resolve service requests. You rely on communication to learn the definition of their problems and also to present the solutions. And even if you solve the customers' problems, if your method of communication gives them a negative feeling, they may never call you back. So high-touch skills are essential to successful customer interaction.

To emphasize this point, consider the results of a survey that addressed why customers stop doing business. The purpose of the survey was to determine the reasons for lost accounts and to answer the question, "Why does a customer change from one supplier to another supplier?"

Among customers who no longer did business with a given supplier, 1 percent died, (if you are in sales it will always seem higher, but it's just 1 percent); 3 percent moved away; 14 percent formed a new business relationship (some of those are for competitive reasons, like outsourcing and other opportunities), and 14 percent were dissatisfied with the product.

That leaves 68 percent–all of who felt an attitude of indifference from one or more representatives of the supplier. So it's key that we work with our customers in a respectful way and that we learn effective telephone communication skills. While poor communication skills can cause you to lose customers, excellent telephone communication skills can build positive and long-lasting relationships with your customers.

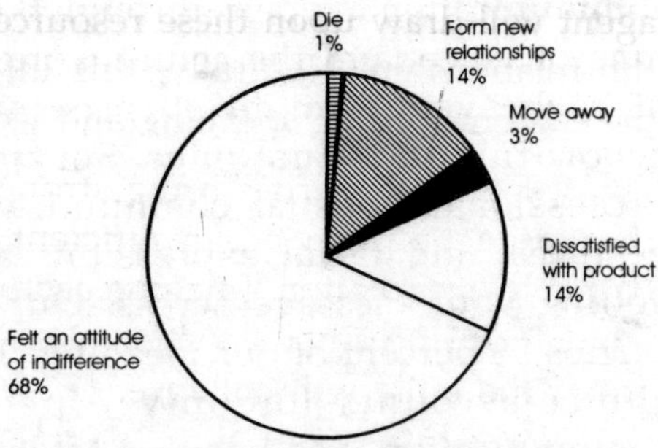

Fig.2. *The results of the study*

HOW TO CREATE OUR IMAGE OVER THE TELEPHONE

We all grew up with telephones, and we all think we know how to use them. We've become so familiar with them, in fact, that many of us have developed bad telephone communication habits.

Because of this, it's important to know and understand the differences between face-to-face communication and telephone communication. Knowing these differences will help you understand how we create our image over the telephone.

THE COMPONENTS OF COMMUNICATION

A term called *Imagineering* has been coined. The Walt Disney Company calls some of their creative people "Imaginers," but that's not all. Combining the words *image*, defined as "a concept or character of something or someone held by the public; a representation to the mind by speech or writing" and *engineer*, defined as, "to plan, construct, or manage by skillful acts", to form the word *imaginer*. The definition for this hybrid word is: "to construct and manage public perceptions through the spoken word; creating either a positive or negative impression." Every time we interact with customers we are *Imagineering*. Whether we care to think about it or not, we are constantly reinforcing or changing the perceptions that others have about us. In a face-to-face situation, communication happens through the avenues of body language, tone of voice, and the actual words used. But the importance of each avenue might surprise you. Figure 2 shows how, according to "Customer Service Skills for Help Desk Professionals" visual communication–your body language, gestures, and facial expressions accounts for 55 percent of getting your message across. Our tone of voice, or attitude, carries 38 percent of our meaning. The content-the actual word choice-accounts for only 7 percent of our face-to-face communication. See below a table on how the three avenues of communication influence face-to-face communication.

The avenues of verbal communication	**Percantage of emphasis face-to-face**
Body language, gesture, facial expression	55 percent
Tone of voice	38 percent
Word content	7 percent

However, as shown in Figure 2, these avenues are weighted much differently when communicating over the telephone. When you're on the telephone, 55 percent of the communication the visual stimulus isn't present. Instead, 85 percent of telephone communication comes across in your *tone*–your attitude, or how you address the customer. And only 15 percent of your message gets across with your words. See below a table on how the three avenues of communication influence telephone communication.

The avenues of verbal communication	**Percantage of emphasis face-to-face**
Body language, gesture, facial expression	0 percent
Tone of voice	85 percent
Word content	15 percent

So, until we get some training, or really think about how powerful the telephone is, we really aren't fully serving our customers. Returning to the concept of *Imagineering*, we need to understand that we create an image each time we interact with a customer over the telephone. Our goal should be to skillfully manage the perceptions we create. To do this, we need to master both listening and speaking skills. □□

Chapter 19

Teaching Communication Skills

What Are Basic Steps Involved In Teaching Communication?

- Review the students major communication skills and how he or she indicates wants and needs from the functional behavioural assessment.
- Choose a communication strategy that will the replace problem behaviour.
- Make sure the communication response is as easy or easier to engage in than the problem behaviour.
- Identify problematic routines where you will begin teaching communication.
- Observe the student to discover the average length of time between the antecedent (triggering event) and the problem behaviour.
- Spend time building rapport by associating yourself with activities, people and things the student values.
- Make sure that when problem behaviour occurs it is more effortful and less efficient than the new communication skill.
- Plan to expand the communication intervention across settings and people as part of a long-term plan.

Why Is Important To Establish Rapport Before Beginning Communication Interventions?

It is important to begin communication training by associating yourself with activities, people, and things that the student values because it will make it easier to prompt a communication response when you begin teaching the student. The goal is to reduce the occurrence of problem behaviours to low levels and to build a positive relationship that will facilitate communication between you and the student. Building rapport means that time is spent developing a positive relationship based upon mutual enjoyment of activities and cooperation without high levels of demands or corrective statements.

Create opportunities for you and the student to spend time together engaging in reinforcing activities that were identified during the functional behavioural assessment. Rapport building is not a one-time event and should be built into interactions at a high enough frequency to maintain the relationship. Once rapport has been established with the student, you will be able to continue with the communication intervention and shape the student's behaviour by prompting communication during the routines you have identified.

Why Is It Important To Know The Length Of Time Between An Antecedent (Triggering Event) And The Problem Behaviour?

It can be helpful to know the length of time between an antecedent (trigger) and the problem behaviour because when at all possible you want to prompt a communication response before problem behaviours occur.

How Can Teaching Communication Become A Strategy For Replacing A Problem Behaviour?

Many different types of behaviours can have the same effect or outcome. A student who is trying to tell you that he needs help on a task may yell at you loudly across the room, raise his hand, or put his head down on the desk and refuse to work. Although these behaviours look different, they can result in the same outcome.

The goal of this intervention is to identify a communication response that will result in the same outcome as problem behaviour. This may mean teaching the student to request a break if she is engaging in problem behaviour to escape from a task, ask for assistance during tasks that are difficult, initiate social interactions to obtain attention, or make a request for an item, event, or activity

Why Is It Important To Consider The Efficiency Of A Communication Intervention?

The student will choose to engage in a behaviour that is most efficient. If the communication behaviour being taught requires more effort, the student may choose to engage in problem behaviour. A number of factors should be considered to make sure a communication intervention will be more efficient than a problem behaviour. When deciding which communication response to teach, consider how much physical effort the student engages in to achieve the same outcome as the problem behaviour. Make sure that the reinforcement a student receives occurs frequently, is powerful enough and is delivered quickly. If a communication intervention is not working well, review these issues related to efficiency and make modifications so that problem behaviour becomes inefficient, ineffective, and irrelevant for the student

How Do You Make Problem Behaviour More Effortful And Less Efficient?

One way to make problem behaviour more effortful and less efficient is to use extinction. When a behaviour that has a history of being reinforced no longer results in reinforcement, behaviour will decrease. For instance, a student may learn over time that if she cries and screams she will gain access to her favourite game. The student's teacher can choose to ignore the student's crying and screaming and immediately reinforce appropriate verbal requests for the game. Over time, the student's crying and screaming will decrease and her verbal requests will increase because this behaviour is more efficient.

Sometimes when using extinction a behaviour may increase for a period of time before it starts to decrease. When extinction begins, the student may actually cry and scream louder and with more intensity before it decreases. This temporary increase in responding that is referred to as extinction burst.

In certain situations, extinction is not possible, especially if a behaviour is dangerous and may lead to safety concerns for the student or others. However, it is still possible to decrease the amount of reinforcement a student receives when engaging in problem behaviour. For instance, if a student pulls a peer's hair to get attention, the teacher can decrease the amount of attention the student receives by quickly redirecting the peer away from the student and reducing the amount attention given to the student during the event from other adults.

□□